THE RETURNING CITIZEN'S SURVIVAL GUIDE

FIRST EDITION

Advice for navigating the barriers and obstacles of re-entry

Frank Patka

SID # 14692795

ISBN 979-8-88851-089-6 (Paperback)
ISBN 979-8-88851-090-2 (Digital)

Covenant Books
11661 Hwy 707
Murrells Inlet, SC 29576
www.covenantbooks.com

To Caleb Goodpasture. You would've liked this one.

CONTENTS

FOREWORD

I met Frank while he was still in prison. It was about a year before his release. I was a dean for the local community college, overseeing the education program at the prison. I was introduced to Frank because he was leading a toastmasters group and was always looking for people willing to come and speak to the group. He immediately invited me to speak at an upcoming meeting.

Administrators and guards at the prison thought highly of Frank Patka. Rather than blend in with the crowd, he volunteered for various leadership roles and acted as a spokesman and advocate for inmates. He taught classes about prosocial behavior and was constantly recommending self-help books to other inmates. Prison officials viewed Frank as a model inmate, but I found out later that this wasn't always the case.

Five years earlier, Frank entered prison as an angry, bitter, and rebellious young man. He fought the system, ignored the rules, and ended up in the hole more often than most prisoners. What changed? A corrections officer had an honest and direct conversation with Frank and recommended a book to him. The book changed Frank's life. He adopted the goals and recommendations from the book and worked diligently to put them into practice. I don't think he questioned the validity of the book. He just believed it to be true and started following the plan. He read other similar books and just kept pushing forward as if success was his only option.

Upon his release, Frank met with me and asked me to mentor him while he reestablished his life back in society. Frank was even more passionate about the concepts in the books he had read and was determined to integrate the ideas into his own life. As I met with Frank over the past five years, I realize that there are just a few simple things that contributed to his success and ultimately resulted in this book.

- He worked within the community, advocating for prison reform and assisting his fellow returning citizens.
- He was constantly asking friends and acquaintances for help and support.
- He had a passion for mentoring and being mentored.

This book comes from someone who has been there and survived re-entry. He genuinely wants to help others. His passion is contagious. He found a practical way and a prioritized method for restarting life on the outside. I highly recommend this book as a road map for your re-entry.

Sincerely,
Jerry Schulz, mentor and friend

PREFACE

When I was released from prison, I had many fears about returning to society. *Will I be able to find a place to live? Will someone hire me? What are people going to think when they find out I was in prison? Are they going to turn me away because of my past? Am I going to be able to fit in?*

The process of returning back to the community has many obstacles and barriers. Overcoming them requires your personal commitment to change and a willingness to do whatever it takes to succeed. Some of the barriers are unfair and unjust, but it is your responsibility to overcome them.

To successfully complete parole and create the life you want, you will need to set goals and accomplish them. Examples of important goals include:

- Finding employment
- securing a safe place to live
- developing prosocial hobbies and relationships
- building financial independence

Overcoming barriers and obstacles is not easy. *You must be prepared when embarking on any journey.* The objective of this guide is to help you prepare for the journey.

INTRODUCTION: SUCCESSFUL RE-ENTRY

It's the day we obsess about the most while serving time: *the day we walk out of the gate as a "free" person.* Whether you served a short sentence of a year or two or served many years of your life behind bars, the day you walk out of prison feels like the *first day of the rest of your life!* However, this "first day of the rest of your life" is only the next step in your journey to freedom.

A person's chances of successfully returning to their community after prison are improved greatly when the person prepares while they are still in prison. Preparing for re-entry requires building trusting relationships with the people who can help you when you release. I know this because I successfully navigated the re-entry challenges after serving seventy months in prison.

I paroled to a safe and healthy place because I earned my sister's trust while still in prison with the work I was doing to change old habits. She and my brother-in-law watched my behavior while I was in prison and determined I could move in with them when I was released.

My father gave me an employment opportunity because he saw me change from a common criminal to a business-minded individual.

I was offered a chance to be mentored by someone who had seen my actions as a leader while in prison, and he believed I was worth investing his time to support my goals and dreams.

Preparing for your successful re-entry by establishing trusting relationships with family and friends while in prison greatly increases your chances of achieving freedom outside of prison.

*****

First, let's define *"successful re-entry."*

Most correctional and re-entry organizations use three years to measure recidivism or *"the tendency for a convicted criminal to reoffend."* These are measured in what is called "recidivism rates." However, not reoffending is only one part of a successful re-entry from prison. A successful re-entry also includes these foundational achievements:

- *Earning a steady income*
- *Affording a safe and consistent place to live*
- *Access to food, clothing, health care, and other resources*
- *Developing healthy relationships*
- *Finding and maintaining fulfilling hobbies*
- *Establishing goals or purpose in life*
- *Having an understanding of how to live within the community or who to turn to for guidance when there is a misunderstanding*

This guide was written to help you prepare for the day you hit the gate because I believe you deserve the best shot at this opportunity we call *re-entry.* I believe you want to stay out of prison. I believe you want to build healthy relationships. And I believe you want some type of significance in your life. I know because I did when I got out.

Our country is a world leader in incarcerating its citizens. Anyone can easily see the damage caused by sending so many citizens to prison. Families are disrupted and damaged because half of the adults in the United States have had a close family member incarcerated.

I believe we can build prosperous communities if we spend more time focused on offering opportunities for you to prepare to be successful in your return from prison.

This guide is one more resource for you to use to be prepared for your next opportunity.

> "Success happens when *opportunity* meets *preparation*."
> —Hall of Fame NFL coach
> Jimmy Johnson

While you are studying this guide, I suggest reading *The Master Plan* by Chris Wilson. Invest in yourself, your change, and your well-being now; and you will find you have actually invested in your future. That's what happened to me.

If you have questions, shoot me a letter:

Frank C. Patka IV

PO Box 675

Bend, OR 97709

SECTION 1

Commitment to Change

MAKING A PERSONAL COMMITMENT

Change starts with a personal commitment…every day!

Every major transition that happens in our life requires us to change within ourselves. These changes to our lifestyle include adjustments to our behavior, beliefs, habits, routines, and traditions. Consider moving to a different country. This significant transition might demand changes in language, culture, etiquette, and so much more! It is during these moments that life provides us motivation to tinker with who we have been, evaluate our honest discoveries, and make intentional adjustments to improve our experience.

Completing your prison sentence and returning back to the community is a significant transition requiring major changes in the way you think, communicate, and interact with others. These changes are required if you want to experience successful re-entry and long-term freedom. Just like a significant transition requires major changes, major changes require a personal commitment.

Have you ever thought about what commitment means? *Commitment* is defined as *"the state or quality of being dedicated to a cause, activity…a pledge or undertaking."* The definition is epic! It is honorable and reputable. I take it as a compliment if someone describes me as *dedicated*. If we don't make a personal commitment to achieving something, then history shows we are likely going to give up when it gets rough. We make this personal commitment to giving ourselves the best chance to succeed.

Take a moment and think about this statement: *The quality of your future is determined by what you personally commit to today.* Powerful words. Let's read it again, but this time read the statement out loud, *"The quality of my future is determined by what I personally commit to today."*

*****

Your mind is the garden; your personal commitment is the seeds.

In 2011, I was *released* back into the general population after spending the summer in the hole. Pale and defeated, I shielded my eyes from the bright sun with my hand as I walked across the prison complex to the metal stairs. Climbing up two flights, I entered a hallway that had no resemblance to being located in a prison and took a seat and waited for my name to be called. It wasn't long after I sat down when a deep voice gave a shout, "Patka," calling me back to meet my new counselor. I stepped into the office lacking enthusiasm and tired of losing at every turn. What was this staff member going to tell me that all the rest already had?

My defeated attitude was immediately challenged by a wall of green Oregon Ducks memorabilia and a banner proclaiming previous head football coach, Chip Kelly's, motto, "Win the Day!" This impressive display of collegiate loyalty came second only to the presence of the large man waving me in to sit down. Sitting behind the desk was my new counselor, Mr. Morrison, whose size indicated his dedication to bodybuilding. Clearly this was a man of self-worth, something I desperately needed. Uncommon among correctional staff, he was willing to show me how I could also have self-worth. This became evident to me through our ongoing conversations.

I was asked a question that marked a fork in the road of my life's journey. Mr. Morrison asked me, "Do you want to keep doing this prison shit, or do you want to learn something cool?"

He offered me an opportunity to learn the formulas to success, the fundamentals of honest self-analysis, and how to implement that knowledge into application. He spent almost two years as my mentor because he saw something in me I did not see in myself.

This life-changing relationship started with him giving me a book to read called *Think and Grow Rich* by Napoleon Hill. It was from this book that I was first introduced to the concept that our mind is a garden where fresh starts begin. This helped me understand how much our dominating thoughts affect our life, and if they are left unchecked, how easily they can bring our downfall.

In your mind's garden, the personal commitment you choose to make is the seeds of your dreams, desires, and purpose. Your behaviors and habits are the soil in which you will plant your seeds of personal commitment. Like any garden, you will need to feed and tend to it as it grows. How well you care for your garden and the quality of harvest you achieve will be determined by the daily routines of your lifestyle.

This book is to prepare you for re-entry. The success I experienced during re-entry leaned heavily on the changes I made internally. These changes started with tending to the garden in my mind. The rest of the section will show you how to prepare your garden and offer examples from my personal experience to help you along the way. There are going to be plenty of external challenges for you to solve and overcome during re-entry. Negative habits, unhealthy routines, and old desires are only going to make it more difficult to deal with these challenges.

Let's get our hands dirty.

*****

The first part of this guide is all about you and making a commitment to yourself. Yes, you, looking in the mirror (figuratively or literally) and honestly deciding which way to go from here. Be aware of any habit of dwelling on the past when you start digging into your garden. Too many times we try to rewrite the past with "shoulda, woulda, coulda," which will diminish any enthusiasm we have toward our future. Remind yourself, no matter what has happened in your life, you arrived right here. That's done.

When I walked out of prison, I had to deal with the reality that I missed experiences, and doors of opportunity were closed on me. I was not going to be a professional boxer, I missed my sister's wedding and the birth of my first nephew, and I was absent from funerals of loved ones. My employment opportunities were restricted from working in any financial industry job due to the robbery I committed. My housing applications were consistently rejected, reminding me of my past behaviors.

I considered giving up when these barriers and obstacles became overwhelming. However, I weathered the storms of rejection by drawing strength from my personal commitment to be a positive influence in my community when released. My commitment helped me through the challenges and protected the seeds of my dreams, which were about to sprout.

During the first year of my return, I lived with my sister and brother-in-law on their property outside of town. With my nephew newly born, they offered me the option to be a ranch hand to pay for rent. One of my chores was to muck out the paddock or clean out the manure, where the horses lived. Every Saturday, I spent a few hours shoveling manure into a wheelbarrow and removing it from the paddock. I listened to audiobooks and podcasts while brainstorming ideas to fulfill my personal commitment.

These ideas became conversations, which led to opportunities like speaking in front of large audiences about how the correctional system is failing taxpayers and how investing in the health of returning citizens is beneficial for everyone in the community. These presentations earned me an opportunity to give a TEDx talk, which connected me to a man named Lewis Sperber. Lewis helped me launch *Changing Patterns*, which allowed me to fulfill my personal commitment *to be a positive influence in my community upon release*. The mission of Changing Patterns is to reduce recidivism by connecting returning citizens to resources, employment opportunities, and community mentors.

*****

Desire

I've struggled the majority of my life committing to anything. I failed to commit to sports. I failed to commit to jobs. I failed to commit to relationships. My failures all led back to the fact I did not make a personal commitment. If I can't even respect my own commitments, how can I expect anyone else to respect them?

Why did I fail? Because I did not have a strong enough desire to keep my personal commitment. It is not enough to just make any commitment. We need our commitment to being strong enough to hold us up when we feel like giving up. The strength of our commitment is dependent on the depths of our desire.

In middle school, I chose to join the school band and play the trumpet. I wanted to play trumpet because my dad played trumpet. In the beginning, I was excited about this commitment. However, halfway through the year, I noticed how much I disliked carrying the trumpet every day on my walk to school. Then the seasons changed from fall to winter testing the strength of my commitment further. It was not long before I broke weak and quit the band. I quit because my desire was not strong enough to support my commitment.

———

Quick note: If you want to get the most out of your investment, get yourself a journal for the questions and exercises in this book. Now would be a good time to grab it.

———

Consider the commitments you quit. Think about the moment when you gave up. What were the reasons for quitting? Now think about what you cherish most. Is it your family? Is it a dream? For me, it was my freedom. Are the reasons you quit other commitments enough to give up on what you most cherish? I think not.

The strength of our personal commitment depends on the level of desire motivating it. If you could do only *one thing* in your life, what would that be? You will not be able to choose any other career or hobby or activity. You can only do one thing. What do you choose? The answer to that question is a window into your desires.

I would choose to be part of the sport of boxing. My love for boxing was even stronger in my youth. When I was twenty years old, I returned to boxing after taking a couple of years off. I was starting to understand the relationship between success and making a commitment, so I made a personal commitment to compete as an amateur for five more years.

Those years off set me back significantly, and even though I trained hard, I was terrible. I got beat up nightly at practice, only to get beat up worse in competition. In my darkest moments when I started to believe I could never win and thoughts of giving up crept in, my commitment remained steadfast as it was rooted deep in desire.

There were many times I wanted to quit, but my commitment gave me strength when I felt weak. My commitment helped get me up at 5:00 a.m. to run before work. It motivated me to push harder than I believed I could at practice. My commitment willed me to endure training on an empty stomach to make weight. It was my commitment that made sure I kept showing up even after back-to-back losses.

I kept fighting year after year, getting beat up less and less. Then came the breakthrough. I actually started winning more than losing! I won multiple state and regional championships including the Oregon Golden Gloves and earned a chance to compete in the U.S. Trials for a shot at the 2008 Olympics.

Boxing taught me the power of making a personal commitment and how exciting the rewards can be. Even though I was an average boxer at best, I was able to overcome obstacles and earn opportunities to compete with some of the best. This was only possible because my commitment was motivated by desire.

Let's look at what it is *you* want in life so your personal commitment is motivated by desire.

*****

When I bounced off my rock bottom, I had no clue what I wanted in life. All I knew was what I didn't want. I didn't want the life that led me to prison, time in the hole, missing weddings and funerals, and losing friends. Knowing what I didn't want helped me look for what I did want—a different direction for my life.

If you don't know exactly what you want, make a commitment to learning how to be successful in life. Learn universal principles for living a successful life such as financial intelligence, communication and leadership skills, goal setting, and relationship building. Make a commitment to be a positive and prosocial influence.

A commitment to live a prosocial life doesn't mean spending a bunch of time thinking about NOT committing a crime. Living a prosocial life is spending time focused on what you want to accomplish in life and how it can benefit your community. When I use the word *prosocial*, I mean for the good of society which includes the good of you.

Read on and work the exercises in this book, and you will know much more about what you want by the end of this section.

*****

Figuring out what we want is best achieved by tapping into our imagination. When was the last time you consciously used your imagination? For some of us, we have been so entrenched in hopeless negativity that our mind has become trained to only focus on our immediate needs. Our imagination has grown weak with neglect. However, I have good news! Our imagination is a muscle that will get stronger the more we use it.

Who is best at imagining dreams? Children! Man, when I was a kid, you wouldn't believe the worlds I created. I don't even remember being home because I would be lost in a world created in my mind. Let's stretch that imagination muscle out.

Think back to something you desired most as a kid. Write down everything you can remember about this dream. *What was it exactly that you desired? What do you remember about the moments when you would imagine this dream? Did you act it out? Did you tell other people?*

Did you notice any feelings come up during the exercise? When I did this exercise, I remembered how important my dream of playing basketball for the Portland Trail Blazers was to me. I felt a combination of nostalgia and sadness. The feeling of nostalgia was a product of the affection I still have for that younger me with big dreams. The source of sadness is most likely tied to disappointment or regret located in some baggage I have not yet let go of. It will be good for me to come back and to process.

It was important for me to forgive myself and let go of the past so the baggage of regret didn't influence my new garden. If you notice any feelings of shame, sadness, or regret while thinking about the past, then you may have some baggage you are carrying, which could have a detrimental effect on your journey now. Make a note in your journal about any feelings that come up, and consider bringing them up with a counselor or treatment provider.

This exercise of recalling a childhood dream is intended to reactivate your imagination and allow you to intentionally practice using it. However, any exercise involved with recalling our past will include the risk of experiencing uncomfortable feelings. These feelings can trigger negative thinking, which, if left unchecked, will negatively affect the work you are doing in this book.

If you notice a pattern of thinking negatively about yourself and your surroundings, then stop what you are doing and write a *gratitude list*. In my experience, this is the quickest way to interrupt unwanted negative thinking and attitude.

You know what? This seems like a great time to write one right now. Let's take the next few minutes, and write a list of what we are grateful for, who we are grateful for, and anything else that comes to mind.

My Gratitude List
My Job
My nephews and nieces
My business partners and the accountability they provide me
My girlfriend
The opportunities supporting this book and the potential change it will create
Having the freedom to travel
A support system of positive influence rich with experience
Having my needs met
Warm coffee refills at Shari's Diner while I write this gratitude list

That was easy!

Gratitude feels good and is a powerful tool to help you maintain a positive mindset. A positive mindset is especially important when preparing our internal garden. We don't want to let weeds of negativity in our garden. Kill those weeds with gratitude, and understand this powerful truth:

Our thoughts influence our attitude.
Our attitude fuels our imagination and affects the strength of our desires.
Our desires dictate our behavior which creates the life we experience.

Whew, that felt like a lot! Writing this reminds me of the ups and downs experienced during early re-entry and how important it is to pay attention to my thinking. Writing a gratitude list is a great exercise to make a habit to influence positive changes.

Now that we have our mindset saturated with gratitude, let's get back to using our imagination and make a personal commitment to the future.

*****

The following exercises will help you complete this process of making a personal commitment and craft a *personal commitment statement* to memorize and keep close as a constant reminder.

You will recognize the question in *Exercise 1* from the earlier story about my return to boxing. This question will help you identify where your strongest desire lives.

Exercise 2 is a much bigger project where you will want to set aside at least thirty minutes of uninterrupted time to get the most out of the work.

Write the answers in your journal where you have room to describe your answers. If you would find it fun, try adding illustrations to color in your answers.

Exercise 1: Find your desire

- *If you could do only ONE THING in your life, what would that be? If you could be remembered for one thing, what would that be?*
- *What amazing things do you want to do?* Write down all the fun, exciting things you have dreamed of doing.
- *What do you want to be remembered for?*

Exercise 2: Eulogy exercise (Remember: give yourself at least thirty minutes uninterrupted)

This is a great exercise for finding purpose. Imagine you have passed away, and you get to listen to others talk about you at your funeral and the eulogy they will hear. While imagining this scenario, write two different eulogies about yourself.

1. *Eulogy 1: Describe your life if nothing changes.*
2. *Eulogy 2: Describe the life of your dreams.*

Use the following questions below to help you craft your eulogy scenarios. Use your imagination and invest your time into writing this out.

- *Who is reading your eulogy?*
- *How long did you live?*
- *Where did you live?*
- *What is your family like?*
- *Who is in your life? Who is at the funeral?*
- *What were your proud moments?*
- *What were your least proud moments?*
- *What have you accomplished?*
- *What were your hobbies?*
- *How do people remember you?*

Once you have written the two eulogy scenarios down, compare them. Are they similar? Are they vastly different? If they are vastly different, this is a sign the life you are living is not helping you toward the life you want to live. These differences expose areas in your life you need to change. Here are some questions to help you get the most out of this exercise.

- *What differences did you find between your two eulogies?*
- *What is one of the amazing things you would like to accomplish in life that you wrote down in the previous exercise?*
- *What needs to happen for you to make the eulogy of your dreams come true?*
- *What did you learn about yourself while doing these exercises?*

Working these exercises thoroughly will give you insight and direction, which will help you craft your personal commitment. The eulogy of your dreams should be the result of your personal commitment.

*****

Writing your personal commitment

Your personal commitment is a dedication toward achieving the *eulogy of your dreams* and why you are willing to make this dedication. Now it is time to write your personal commitment statement. This is a one or two-sentence statement proclaiming the personal commitment you are making.

When I started Changing Patterns, I had to make a commitment to live a clean life. I wanted to be of service to my community, but it took me making a personal commitment to be someone who could be trusted and would lead others in a positive direction. As long as I kept my personal commitment, I was able to bring community members and returning citizens together to reduce recidivism.

My commitment enabled me to build relationships with people I would never have met had I been behaving in my old routine lifestyle. I have relationships with POs, counselors, and organizational leaders who provided our clients with opportunities to find employment and help them grow into productive community members themselves. It all started with a personal commitment.

I suggest your written personal commitment be a one- or two-sentence statement. Remember, this is just something simple you can put in a visible place or be kept on your person to act as a reminder. Be specific about what change you are committing to and *why* you are making this commitment. Here are some examples of ways to format your sentence to use in developing your own commitment statement:

- "I am making a personal commitment to change_______________, so my family can be proud of me."
- "I, (your name), am making a personal commitment to change ____________ because (what do you care about most)."

Take a few stabs at it. Write a few statements like the examples above in your journal that proclaim your commitment to the new life you are working toward. Play around with your statements until you come up with one you really like. When you are satisfied with your personal commitment statement, write it on a piece of paper that you will keep by your bedside. Read it first thing in the morning and last thing at night. Read and think about your commitment every day until it becomes part of your identity.

Here are some of the benefits of having a personal commitment:

- Regularly reminding yourself of your personal commitment will help you stay focused and dedicated while you fulfill postprison commitments that you may not enjoy.
- If you notice yourself slipping back into old habits or negative thinking, use your personal commitment as a reminder of why you want to avoid backsliding and negative thinking.
- Your personal commitment can be used as a filter to make hard decisions easier. Anytime you find yourself at a fork in the road needing to make a tough decision, ask yourself, "Does this help or hurt my personal commitment?"

The eulogy of your dreams is the seed of your personal commitment. With care and attention, your seeds of personal commitment will grow and produce opportunities for you to achieve the life you want. Keeping your personal commitment in a place you see daily will help you stay focused.

*****

CHANGE STARTS WITH A PERSONAL COMMITMENT...EVERY DAY!

A warning from the future: Failure to keep your personal commitment top of mind and neglecting your garden has disastrous results. I almost lost everything because I let distractions draw my attention away from my personal commitment.

At the time of editing and revising this book, I am personally battling addiction because I became complacent in using my personal commitment statement and chased distractions.

"It's okay to have a good time" is a big f——ing lie for some of us. Look, I love to party, and I know many people in the world love to party. However, some of us can stop and can behave in ways that do not cause harm while others, like myself, can wind up being the last ones left at the party.

Man, it's so easy to start. First, it's a drink at a gathering surrounded by successful people, then it's a friend's birthday or a holiday. The party occasions never stop. There is always something ahead offering a reason to party. I found myself stuck in a loop "wanting and waiting for a break." But there is no break until I commit to stopping, or some outside entity like the cops creates a break for me.

In my experience, it happened gradually. I didn't even smoke weed for months after I got out, but eventually, I did. I didn't fall straight down like *puff, puff, crash*, but my faults snuck up quietly, just like you learn in twelve-step programs: cunning, baffling, and powerful.

We are teased with fool's gold and dreams of euphoric fantasies as tangible as the fog resting in a harbor. You can see it and feel what it could be like, but like the fog, you can never grasp it. The lies that capture your attention are like a mirage of a lighthouse distracting you from the rocks about to destroy your vessel. It's drunk nights pontificating on what could've been which lead to Bloody Mary's before work. It's the cocaine at the party that turned into a daily habit. Soon, the taste becomes palpable in your everyday living—not obnoxious, but ever-present, like someone you hang with every day who causes you to consider: "Are they my friend?"

Before long, you can't tell that the thing comforting you from the upset and complaining people is also the cause of the problems making people upset in the first place. It seems to be the *only* relief for you. It tells you how crazy everyone else is and that you are better off without them. The next thing you know, your only *friend* is also the thing that destroyed you.

It's okay to have a good time, but always recognize where each time can lead. I write about my recent struggles as an example that everyone has to face their own personal challenges. I am using this commitment section to help me focus on my personal change and set my navigation back toward living a prosocial life of purpose. Instead of making a commitment to *not* do drugs or drink, I am making a commitment to focus on finishing this book and supporting opportunities for returning citizens to achieve freedom. You know it worked if you are reading this book.

How does this look in action? Well, any idea proposed, even one to go out and enjoy an evening filled with liquor and laughs, gets filtered through my personal commitment filter.

- Does this idea help me achieve my goals of finishing this book?
- Does it support returning citizens achieving freedom? Or will it delay achieving my goal?
- Does this idea have gray areas which could cause me trouble? Is this an idea I can be proud of?

These questions may seem excessive to consider, but they can be easily answered quickly. When you've developed the habit to use your commitment as a filter to make decisions, this process happens at the speed of thought.

Here's the thing, we make personal commitments every day even though we might not think about it. Every single decision we make is a commitment. Some are small commitments like deciding what to eat, while others could be incredibly impactful like deciding to leave a job or move to another city. These are all commitments.

The combination of all of your thoughts and actions got you to the place you are right now! Your life right now is experiencing the results of what you committed to in the past whether you did it on purpose or unconsciously. Why not make these decisions purposely?

Achieving freedom demands from us a personal commitment to change. What must we change? We must commit to changing everything that will hurt our ability to fulfill our personal commitment. We must commit to changing the habits associated with harmful behaviors. We must commit to changing the old, destructive patterns and replacing them with a new, constructive routine lifestyle.

This commitment must be made every day to avoid risking the consequences of complacency. The consequences of our complacency are mentioned in an all too familiar mantra, "Jails, institutions, and death."

*****

New commitments require new habits

Our habits make up the quality of the soil in our mind's garden where the seeds of our personal commitment are planted. After working hard to choose the seeds of your personal commitment, the last thing you want to do is plant them in bad soil. You can have the highest quality seeds (best intentioned personal commitment), but if you plant them in nutrient-deficient soil or hard clay, these seeds will be useless.

For many of us, our past shows that we habitually made unhealthy decisions. If these unhealthy decisions have been part of our routine for a significant amount of time, then the soil of our garden will be unfit for our new seeds. It will require us to tend to the soil which consists of our habits.

Charles Duhigg writes in his book *The Power of Habit* that we must *replace* our habits. We cannot just quit them. Before we can replace them, we need to evaluate our habits and determine which to keep and which to replace. We do this through an exercise called habit tracking.

Habit tracking is a tedious activity demanding that you pay close attention to all your behaviors over time. Follow these steps to properly track and evaluate your habits:

1. Carry with you a piece of paper and pen over the next few days. Each time you notice a habit, write it down. If you are having a hard time identifying habits as they happen, start by documenting obvious ones like *brushing your teeth, taking a shower, doing laundry, and lifting weights*. Eventually, you will start to notice less tangible habits like *how you*

react to bad news or rejection, differences in the way you talk to certain people, and what your morning and evening routines look like. Do this for a minimum of one day, but I recommend continuing this exercise for a few days (three) to get as accurate of a collection as possible.

2. Evaluate the collection of habits you have tracked and split them up into two groups:
   a) habits that help
   b) habits that harm
3. On a separate piece of paper, write the list of *harmful habits* in a column on the left side
4. On the right side of the paper, write the list of *healthy habits* you will use as replacements for the *harmful habits*. For example, if you do not want to use drugs or alcohol or maybe quit smoking cigarettes, you will need to replace the activity with a contradicting one like running or working out. See the following example:

Harmful Habits	Healthy Replacement Habits
Sleeping in	Got bed an hour earlier
Smoking cigarettes	Run daily
Eating too much junk food	Buy healthy food options

We need to replace harmful habits with new ones that influence us to make healthy decisions. Make health and wellness goals part of your commitment. Your body is the only vehicle for this part of life's journey.

Our commitment and direction will offer insight into what supporting habits we can use as replacements. If you have a habit of watching too much TV but made a personal commitment to become a personal trainer, then you can replace TV time with time studying for your International Sports Sciences Association certification.

Replacing your unhealthy habits with healthy alternatives takes intentional focus, dedication, and persistence. I recommend reading

The Power of Habit as a resource to better understand the nature of habits and how to take control of your habits.

*****

You are preparing for a major change, returning back to the community. This change is stressful and brings with it challenges, barriers to navigate, and obstacles to overcome. Your commitment is going to be tested. There are going to be moments when you feel like quitting. I want to take this moment to tell you with all certainty that no matter how hard it gets, do not allow yourself to give up.

One of the worst habits in life is the habit of giving up. In my entire life of good and bad decisions, the decisions that held me back most in life were times I gave up. The most painful moments in my life were when close friends gave up their life.

What makes us give up and quit? There are some really good reasons why someone quits. Many of these reasons are external:

- "I quit because I don't like my boss."
- "I didn't want to carry the instrument to school."
- "The French teacher sucked."
- "He always wanted to argue about everything."

Finding a reason to quit is easy, but if you dig down to the root cause of quitting, you will find the reason for quitting has everything to do with you and your desires. The reason any of us quit is that we are no longer personally committed to the goal or activity. We are 100 percent responsible for everything we quit. Yes, it's your fault you quit just like it is my fault I quit. Look, I know life is not black and white but instead many shades of rationalization and justification. I get there can be drastic reasons, which can knock us off our track. However, that *is* part of life.

The time is now. Your future, your happiness, and your freedom depend on you making a strong personal commitment. Your personal commitment depends on the level of desire in which it is made. No one escapes the outside forces that become obstacles in our journey. But those who make a personal commitment motivated by a strong desire will be better prepared to withstand the tests of life and weather the storms.

The people you read about, look up to, listen to, and admire for what they have achieved *all* made personal commitments stronger than any reason to quit. They all made personal commitments motivated by desire. It all starts here.

Before you get the opportunity to face a challenge that makes you question your commitment, I want you to remember when you pushed past your expectations. Think of the time you accomplished something you wanted. What did you achieve? Why did you commit to achieving it? What were the results? Write about these experiences in your journal.

If you notice your commitment slipping or feel your desire is not what it used to be, open up those stories you just wrote down and read them for inspiration. Your own past can motivate the present and change your future. These experiences are evidence of the power associated with making a personal commitment. This commitment is one of the most intimate agreements you make and will have a lasting influence on the rest of your life.

As you continue through this book, pay attention to how your personal commitment evolves and becomes part of you. Consider the significance of this act of dedication. What you have done here in this section is a pivot point in beginning your greatest achievements. This isn't light work. This is *life* work.

*****

The seeds of your personal commitment are germinating in this early stage. You know how to tend to the soil in your garden by pulling the weeds of bad habits. You may need to till the soil in your garden if negative behaviors of your past have left unwanted conditions through seasons of neglect.

It is time to set your routine to water your garden while you work on preparing to overcome the external obstacles and barriers of your upcoming re-entry. Your routine is the reason your garden will grow. You can prepare everything perfectly and plant the seeds you want in nutrient-rich soil. But if you do not water your garden, your dreams will not grow.

Use your new habits to set your routine lifestyle. Use the *one-week schedule* in the *Resource Section* to write down all of your regular activities including your new habits. Don't forget to include time to work on preparing for re-entry. You'll notice that the schedule does not go past 10 p.m. I set that up because out here, outside of working a graveyard shift, there is nothing going on past 10 p.m. that I want or need to be involved with.

I've heard people tell me that they have their best inspiration at night. I get it, and if you are using that time for yourself and your betterment, then all the power to you. However, if the only thing you are doing past 10 p.m. is watching TV, I encourage you to use this time to adjust your routine to wake up earlier. Being active at night is old behavior for most of us. Best to replace it with the opposite behavior.

I've been out here for a while, and I can tell you that there isn't anything healthy for us going on after 10 p.m. The TV isn't even worth it, so get some sleep. And if you are thinking that you need more hours, add them in the morning when the energy is fresh and the rested are stirring.

———

You've made your personal commitment to change. You know you need to make this commitment every day in to overcome the challenges ahead. *If you schedule in your routine a daily activity of acknowledging your personal commitment*, then it won't be long before this most important action will become a habit requiring little to no thought. This leads us to the garden of our desires when we apply the routine lifestyle properly.

If your personal commitment influences positive thinking and behavior, motivates prosperous achievement, and provides fulfilling life experiences of freedom, then you know your routine lifestyle is laid out with healthy habits. Continue your routine with a dedication to keeping your schedule as consistent as possible. In due time, your routine will become an automated action requiring very little thinking or effort to maintain.

This automated healthy routine lifestyle improves your life each day. An automated routine frees up your mind so you are able to consider new opportunities that offer the potential for growth in knowledge, experience, and prosperity.

*****

Re-entry is the house; you are the foundation

Proper preparation and regular care of your garden will produce a harvest best described as *freedom*! *The fruits of your harvest feed you during your journey toward the direction that defines freedom for you.* These fruits, having incredible value, will earn you the life of your dreams, which will produce a sense of freedom that words cannot describe.

The work in this section determines the strength of the foundation you will build your metaphorical house of re-entry. The success or failure during early re-entry is going to depend on the quality of work in this section. Before spending too much time celebrating the completion of this section, I recommend going back through to review what you learned and to look for areas you may not have done your best.

Your focused dedication to doing the highest quality work in this section will be evident when you weather the storms of life. These storms could be losing a job, breaking up with your significant other, an unforeseen accident, or even an unfair hand dealt to you. Life is full of events that are unavoidable and beyond our control, but what you can control is the fortitude of your personal commitment and the house of re-entry it supports.

Many have failed to complete supervision, returned to prison, and even lost their lives due to a storm causing the collapse of their poorly built structure. Avoid this awful experience by doing the work right here and right now!

*****

CONCLUSION: WHATEVER IT TAKES!

You can achieve all those great things you wrote down, but you need to be willing to do whatever it takes to get there. The journey isn't always pretty, and it is going to have plenty of moments, which will test your commitment. Those who make it are the ones who are willing to do *whatever it takes*. Whatever it takes isn't permission to do things shady or off the books. Whatever it takes means you are willing to do things you don't want to do to move forward.

It might mean taking a job you don't enjoy to get income while you search for a better job. It means doing what your PO tells you to do even though you may not see any benefit. It means ending relationships that are not helping you no matter how difficult it sounds.

I want to help you, which is why I wrote this guide, but most importantly, YOU have to want to help yourself. I am going to beat this drum over and over again because I have watched returning citizen after returning citizen give up because they expected people to do the work for them or they weren't willing to do whatever it takes.

This may be the most important thing I can tell you, my friend. No one, and I mean *no one*, is going to do the work for you. You have to do it. And you have to earn it. No one owes you anything. You are where you are because of the actions and decisions you have made. You are responsible for where you are. This is GREAT news because when we are responsible for something, we can take control of it.

Take responsibility for your situation and the problems that come with it, so you can take credit for the solutions. All you have to do is whatever it takes.

*****

As this section comes to a close, I want to ask you to take a moment and pause…

We can get in such a hurry that sometimes we forget to celebrate small milestones. One of the rewards of making these changes is gaining a better understanding of yourself and an increased awareness of life as it happens. The more intentional we are in how we participate in life, the better we can understand how to navigate the journey.

What you have experienced while working through this section is called living life on purpose. You aren't just going with the flow or being driven by outside influence. For the time we have spent together, you have made a conscious effort for the betterment of yourself for an intended purpose. Make this purposeful way of living a routine.

As you go through the following sections, don't forget to check back in on your garden. It is wise to frequently check in with your habits, routine, and mindset in these early stages of change. These new habits need time to establish—sixty-six days on average to make a behavior a habit. Use the tools you've learned in this section regularly to keep yourself accountable to your personal commitment.

It can be easy to get distracted by the project immediately in front of you and forget the important responsibility you have tending to your garden. Of everything in this book, your garden is the most important piece. It is the foundation on which the rest of your life is built.

After completing each section, run through this question checklist:

Mindset:

- Have I noticed any negative thoughts show up in my day? If so, what is the nature of these thoughts? What am I doing when these thoughts arise? Who am I around when I notice these negative thoughts?
- What is my plan to get control of these unwanted thoughts, so I can focus on improving my life and preparing for my release?

Personal commitment:

- Is there anything about my personal commitment I should change based on the new information I have learned?
- What feelings do I notice about my personal commitment?
- How would I rate my confidence in fulfilling my personal commitment? Is my confidence improving or decreasing since the last time I answered this question? Why or what do I think has caused this change?
- Habits:
- What is my progress report on replacing the old habits with new ones?
- Which habits were easiest for me to change? Why?
- Which habits have been the hardest for me to change? Why?
- What negative habits have I been avoiding to start changing? Why am I procrastinating on starting this process?
- Do I notice any changes in my day-to-day experiences with the changes I have made?
- What can I do better in this process? Am I willing to make a commitment to this improvement?

SECTION 2

Survival Checklist

Housing
Employment
Transportation
Food, clothing, and hygiene
Documentation
Bank account
Health care
Support system

*****

BUILDING A FOUNDATION

In order to get to freedom, we must survive the journey. Like building a house, building a life starts from the ground up. You have to build a foundation before you can build the roof.

If you don't have food, you aren't going to care about the great things you wrote about in section 1. You are going to care about how hungry you are and where to find your next meal.

It is common for returning citizens to think in terms of one-offs, meaning to get something just once. *"If I can get the next meal, I can live to the next meal."* This is a habit commonly developed through substance abuse. Chasing the next high is a one-off lifestyle.

This is a very important pattern to change if you want to achieve freedom.

Freedom comes to those who invest in tomorrow through today's actions.

Remember, *we are living in the results of our past actions.*

Every action and decision we made led us to this point. We exist in the consequences of our past. For example, I committed an armed robbery in 2010. In 2015, I wasn't committing armed robbery anymore, but I was still in prison living in the consequence of that action.

Remember this concept as we start this journey of personal commitment to change. We make these changes and expect immediate results, but the changes today are actually investments in the future. We aren't going to see the results right away.

Yeah, but I'm trying to survive today. What good is an investment for tomorrow if I don't make it through today?

I get it. It is hard to consider your future when the present seems bleak or overwhelming. I understand what it feels like and what it takes to overcome the challenges of returning to the community. I wrote this guide so you can handle the present while still investing in your future freedom.

We must change our thinking from getting that next meal to creating a way to get meals constantly flowing into our life. You can use this checklist to help you build your foundation.

*****

How to use the checklist

Each item on the *Returning Citizen's Survival Guide checklist* is a cornerstone and foundation of the life you want to build. They are the first targets you must hit, so you can be secure when it's time to chase your freedom. And, hey, feelings of freedom come with completing this checklist.

For example, a full-time job provides a consistent means to pay rent and live in a place you can afford. Stable housing supports your journey toward freedom and your personal commitment to change. With a full-time job, you have a consistent means for a safe place to live.

Don't actually check off an item until you have it as a constant in your life. Work your way through this list while using your personal commitment as a guide in making decisions. Also, if you have questions to ask or stories you'd like to share, please send a letter to:

Changing Patterns
PO Box 675
Bend, OR 97709

If you have released or have access to an email, feel free to email mc at info@changingpatternsinc.org.

*****

There are eight main checklist items in this guide. Each item is considered a baseline or survival item. In order to live a free life, you must be able to obtain, understand, and secure consistency for each one of these items.

*****

HOUSING

Obtaining safe housing has been one of the hardest challenges for me and most returning citizens. It is also one of the most important foundation pieces to achieving freedom. So many other pieces come together once you can secure a safe place to call home.

There is a good chance you are reading this and have no idea where you are going to live when you get out. Since getting out of prison, I have had to overcome several challenges and obstacles to achieve a steady and safe place to live. Here's how I earned places to live:

While in prison, I spent much of my time replacing my bad habits with healthier ones and spent years proving to my family they could trust me. Luck played a small factor in that my sister and her husband have done life rather wisely and were able to offer me a place to live the first year I got out.

You need to be working on housing with a release counselor and healthy friends and family to find an approved place to live. The sad truth is, obtaining housing can be a challenge and may continue to be for many years for returning citizens. The sooner you can secure an approved housing opportunity, the better.

After my first year out, I moved into a room I rented from a friend. I'll say this now, and I'll go deeper into it later in the guide, but *one of the most important skills you can develop is networking and building healthy relationships. My housing opportunities were a result of developing healthy relationships.*

Our society prides itself on making sure people account for their mistakes and actions but fails to support those who have paid the price. Our society is great at punishing our citizens for doing something wrong but lacks heavily in providing opportunities for returning citizens to earn a place as productive community members. Don't we want all our community members healthy, safe, and prosperous?

This failure to provide opportunity is so highly evident in our country's housing system.

If you are going to be released to a community where Section 8 housing considers those with a criminal background, consider yourself lucky. There are many communities where people who carry the scarlet letter *F* do not qualify for low-income housing.

The reality is that until more people invest in housing opportunities for returning citizens, it's going to be a tough hurdle to overcome. But it's possible!

Hopefully, you are able to secure, at the very least, some transitional housing. A transitional house isn't ever the dream situation, but it can be a great launch pad if you use it correctly.

If you aren't sure where to start looking for housing options, start by asking for help from trusted people such as

- Counselor
- Prosocial, clean family or friends

- Oxford housing (or other twelve-step sponsored housing)
- Local re-entry/transitional housing
- Have someone search on Google/Facebook/Craigslist for rooms for rent

Private renters are most likely your best shot. Property management companies *will take your application and your money,* but they will *almost never* accept you as a renter.

Also, be careful of scams. NEVER send an application to rent a place via email! Applications contain personal information, which you want to manage closely. Only share your personal information after you have verified the place and met the person from whom you are going to rent.

In a pinch, the local homeless shelter—*whatever it takes* to be safe—I have also slept in my vehicle in desperate times (but this is NOT ideal).

The truth is, the housing system is built to keep you out. Our society wants you to be successful, just not in their neighborhood. You are going to have to work ten times harder to find a place to live than anyone else. However, you can start doing things now to increase your housing opportunities in the future.

*****

Things to know

- One-third of your income is the general consideration for housing costs. If you make $3,000/month, you could be considered to rent at $1000/month at the most. Consider your gross (before taxes) monthly income before applying to rent.
- You may need a first and last month's rent plus a security deposit when entering into a rental agreement. Saving money to prepare for these large expenses is important. Make it a goal to save as much as possible for this expense. $3,000 is a minimum target to set for securing housing.

- Prepare a list of references who will speak about your character regarding housing.

Raising money

There are many ways to acquire income. We are familiar with earning money through work and asking for money as a loan or gift. However, for those who are willing to get creative, *raising money* for initial housing costs is a great way to connect with your support system and offer them an opportunity to invest in your success upon release.

Think about what you can offer to those who provide initial financial support. If someone donates $200, what will you give them after you get out? Consider what you might give as a *return on investment* to those who help support you.

Crowdfunding is an online way for people to contribute and support an event or situation. Ask someone in your support system if they would be willing to set up a crowdfunding opportunity in support of your return to the community.

Here are some of the top crowdfunding sites:

- <u>Kickstarter</u>
- <u>Indiegogo.com</u>
- <u>GoFundMe.com</u>

Raising money is a task to be taken seriously. If you do raise money, be grateful for the sacrifice of those who donated. They worked hard for their money, and their support is an example of their love and belief in your success. Don't let them down. Be humble. Be grateful. And look for ways to pay them back once you get out and settled.

You can't save TOO much money! No matter how much you raise, how much you earn, and how much you save, it will never be enough. Life out here is expensive for returning citizens fresh out of prison.

The more you save while you are locked up, the more leverage you will have to navigate the barriers and obstacles of re-entry.

Trust this statement: *When I was released from prison, I immediately regretted the canteen purchases near my release date.*

One can justify any canteen purchase. But in prison, money is mostly for entertainment. On the contrary, money is an important navigation tool in society. There is no soup, cheese squeeze, or meat stick in prison more valuable than that dollar out in society. It is up to you to decide how much you are willing to sacrifice to save for release.

Create a budget and determine how much of your income you would like to set aside for release. Stick with your plan. If you are going to save 10 percent of your income for release, stand by this every month. Don't spend the money even though you will want to as it grows. Trust me, when you get out, you will have wished you saved more.

*****

Build your credit score

I am going to dive further into the importance of credit later in this book, but I am introducing it here because of the significant influence your credit score has on securing housing options.

I learned about the influence credit has on your ability to secure housing the hard way. I was not responsible with my credit privileges, which resulted in a low credit score and many denials for housing through property management companies.

The good news is if you have been in prison longer than six years, then most likely your past delinquent accounts (if you had any) have fallen off due to the statute of limitations. In most cases, the statute of limitations is seven years. This means, you may be starting fresh when you get out, which is an incredible opportunity.

Research everything you can about building credit and the apps that are available to you today to help monitor and manage your credit score. A few things to know for when you get out:

- Find an app to keep you informed. I use one called Credit Karma on my phone to be able to view and manage my credit score. There are many apps offering credit monitoring. Choose the one you like.
- *Myth:* Checking your credit score will hurt it.
- *Truth:* You can receive updates and changes to your score as they happen using online resources like Credit Karma without getting a negative hit on your score. Even a hard inquiry—where your credit is checked to get a car, house, or credit card—only has a minor effect on your score.

A challenge to the willing and brave: *Learn to use credit cards as a tool for building credit so one day you can own property others pay you to live in (long-term thinking).*

Using credit cards to build your credit is a fantastic way to watch your score climb faster than you expected. It also takes a strong discipline to build the habit of staying below your means with credit cards.

The most important part of this strategy: You must pay off your card every month!

You are using credit cards to *build your credit*. Make a personal commitment to use your credit card to purchase only things you would normally purchase: food, gas, pay a bill, then pay off your card every month. When you pay your card off each month, you won't have to pay interest, you won't go overbudget, and you will build your credit score fast.

Also, you create a safety net in case of emergencies. As you responsibly build your credit, you will be given larger lines (amounts) of credit. Having these significant amounts of credit available is a great relief if you experience an emergency, like losing a job, surprise medical problems, or an unforeseen emergency, like your car breaking down. Having the credit available to cover these costs saves you from having to use your cash supply.

WARNING: It takes extreme discipline to carry a credit card around and not use it. There can be a *very* painful lesson that comes from misusing a credit card. I know, from personal experience that short-term gratification purchases can severely hurt you in the long run.

If you are going to utilize credit cards in your journey, I suggest making a personal commitment along these lines:

I am making a personal commitment to use credit cards ONLY as a means to build my credit. I am making a personal commitment to pay my credit card off every month no matter what. I have made this personal commitment to building my credit because I know someday I am going to need good credit just to live in a house!

TIP: Leave your credit card at home when going out with friends.

*****

I can't stress this enough: Building your credit will make people take you seriously. More people are willing to look past one's criminal history when they have a great credit score. It will take time to build, but it is worth the reward.

If you find yourself starting to overuse your card, ask for help from a trusted person in your life, someone who is part of your *support network*.

Build a support network

Nobody achieves anything great without the help of others. Building a network of prosocial community members will create a safety net for you when times get tough. You are going to want and need the support of your community to lean on in order to achieve freedom.

I have depended on board members, friends, and family for temporary living situations in my journey. In fact, as I write this book, I am in transition with my housing situation. I moved out of my house, which was attached to the business I managed. The current housing situation where I live makes it hard for anyone right now since we have a low vacancy rate, which means it is exceptionally hard for a returning citizen like me. And I've been out for over four years!

Thankfully, I have built a support network, which I will touch on more later in the book. Building a support network starts with sticking to your personal commitment to change behaviors and attitudes and make decisions that earn the trust of community members.

Goals and targets:

Here is a CHECKLIST to help you plan. I have added examples, and you can add other priorities and targets along with a date you'd like to complete them.

Item	Date
• *Identify approved housing options available through a release counselor* • *Contact housing options for applications* • *Locate emergency housing options for backup (homeless shelter)* • ____ • ____ • ____	• _________________________ • _________________________ • _________________________ • _________________________ • _________________________ • _________________________

*****

EMPLOYMENT

I have good news for you: The employment world is more apt to hire returning citizens than ever before! The employment landscape has evolved in many ways. People are changing jobs much more often. The average time one stays with a job currently is about four and a half years versus an average of more than twenty years in the past. There also seems to be a common complaint about people not working hard enough. That means a little hard work goes a long way for employers.

If you do not have a job, then finding a job is your job. If you spend your time searching for a job, like you would be working a forty-hour job, I guarantee, you will find a job before the week is over. Will it be the exact job you want? Maybe not on the first run, but I know this: There is always a job somewhere for someone willing to do it. And it may surprise you, but it's easier to get a better job when you have a job.

Here's the deal, I have seen returning citizens fail to get a job because they just waited for someone to get it for them. Utilizing resources like the state-run employment department or staffing services is great to get connections. But don't just wait for them to call you, get out there and hunt!

Here is a story of a returned citizen I had the opportunity to work with. He was walking himself to our local government staffing agency for a meeting with an employment counselor when they called to cancel the appointment due to the COVID-19 pandemic.

He turned around and was walking home when he noticed a bunch of construction trucks driving in and out of a lumberyard. He noticed phone numbers on the sides of the trucks and called one of them.

The first number he called was a company that hired him right there on the spot!

Be proactive and get yourself a job. Utilize resources, but don't wait for anyone else to find you a job. Take responsibility, and get yourself a job!

Goals and targets:

Here is a CHECKLIST to help you plan. I have added examples, and you can add other priorities and targets along with a date you'd like to complete them.

*****

Employment checklist

Résumé. You should have a current, up-to-date résumé no longer than two pages. I suggest getting everything you can onto one page. Your résumé needs to be tailored for the job you are applying for while highlighting why you are the right person for the job. Make the résumé specific for the position.

Tip: Ask your transition coordinator or release counselor for a résumé template to use as an example. I also included one of my résumés on the resources page for you.

References. You want to have at least three nonfamily members who are credible references who know you are going to use them on job applications. *A "credible" reference is someone who has a good reputation, a history of experience, and the information to provide you with an outstanding reference.*

Notify or ask someone *before* you put them down as a reference so they can be prepared to offer supporting information. Provide your references with a copy of your résumé.

Interviewing. Another thing to consider is how you interview. Interviewing is a skill in communication. It is important to be ready to confidently advocate for yourself and explain why you are the best person for the job.

Hopefully, you will be able to go through a transitions or release class, which will offer interview tips and a chance to practice. Some answers you will want to prepare are

- Why you have a large gap in your employment
- How you are going to explain your criminal background
- What skills or strengths will you showcase?

Email. Email is the main tool for professional communication. You should have an email in one of these formats and I recommend a Gmail account: *firstnamelastname@gmail.com, firstname.lastname@ gmail.com, firstinitiallastname@gmail.com.*

If you have a common name, you may need to add a number. Do not pick *420* or *666* or *69*. This is your professional signature.

Give yourself a chance, and don't use your old <u>puffpuffpass420@</u> <u>hotmail.com</u>.

Phone. You will need a mobile phone; get one! There may be resources in your community that offer some sort of phone plan. I have yet to have a client get to us without a phone. This seems to be the easiest and first resource people acquire when released.

Transportation. You will need to consider your available transportation options as you search for employment. Are you able to get to work? Have you established some form of consistent transportation? Do you have a bike, or are you taking public transportation? Do you have your driver's license and a reliable vehicle?

Learn LinkedIn. LinkedIn is a social network platform for professionals. It is a unique opportunity where people can connect and develop professional relationships in an employment-oriented online service.

LinkedIn is a great tool to introduce yourself to people who may be interested in working with you on a professional level. It is great if you have a sales job.

Set up your profile to make a great first impression, and take courses on how to utilize it to the full extent. Your reputation is valuable here, so do your best to maintain one that has integrity and follows through. The professional world does not make time to waste time.

Look for mentors, people to learn from, and potential business partners and associates while learning what new and exciting things are happening in the professional world.

Other employment considerations. Do you consider the jobs that you are no longer qualified to do because of the nature of your crime? I've had to turn down job opportunities in the insurance and financial industry because of my robbery charge.

Short-term vs long-term employment. Is this a job you want to stay at for a long time, or is it a temporary situation to get you started? Some jobs are just means to an end, a way to pay rent. Others are opportunities or stepping stones toward a career you may be pursuing. Avoid being trapped in a job you don't love by understanding what the position is providing. If it is a temporary job, a means to an end, then don't stop looking for a better job after you get hired. Make sure to leave a job on good terms for references in the future.

Resources available. There are local staffing services and state-run employment departments available to help you find a job. Our organization, Changing Patterns, partners with WorkSource of Oregon to increase employment opportunities for returning citizens. There is also a plethora of online services available for you:

- https://linkedin.com
- https://www.simplyhired.com
- https://www.ziprecruiter.com
- https://www.glassdoor.com
- https://www.indeed.com
- https://www.monster.com
- https://www.craigslist.com
- https://www.facebook.com

If you would like more information about looking for employment, how to set up a résumé, or tips on interviewing, send me a letter inquiring about employment.

Goals and targets:

Here is a CHECKLIST to help you plan. I have added examples, and you can add other priorities and targets along with a date you'd like to complete them.

Item	Date
• *Updated résumé (print and digital)* • *Professional email (see page 36)* • *Current physical ID* • *Accepted Social Security number* • *Create transportation plan* • _______________ • _______________ • _______________	• _______________ • _______________ • _______________ • _______________ • _______________ • _______________ • _______________ • _______________

****

TRANSPORTATION

As I mentioned earlier, the topic of your transportation must be considered with the many decisions you need to make.

- If you get a job, how will you get there on time each day?
- How are you going to get to your PO visits or to treatment classes?
- What happens if you need to go out of town or meet up with friends?

Many of us do not get out of prison with a driver's license and a vehicle. We must find other means to travel and be willing to do *whatever it takes* to make sure we get where we need to go on time.

If you are lucky enough to live in an area with effective public transportation, then all you need to do is focus your efforts on learning the routes and timing so you are not late for work or appointments. Public transportation is a learned skill because you have to know how long it takes from point A to B. If you aren't familiar with your local public transportation, I suggest spending a day traveling the routes to learn where each goes and the time it takes to get places. This might be costly up front but not as costly as being late for work or missing an appointment.

Also, many state department resources and transitional programs offer transportation vouchers for returning citizens.

Tip: *When you get out, learn how to use* Google Maps *if you haven't already. Google Maps will give your routes to your destination and approximate arrival times with options for walking, riding a bicycle, or driving.*

*****

If you live in an area like Central Oregon, where I am from, public transportation may not be the most reliable or readily available. If you don't have a license, it will be important to come up with a *transportation plan.* I recommend finding a resource to get a bicycle. Bicycles are relatively inexpensive to get. (You don't need a thousand-dollar bike to get yourself to work.)

If you have a suspended license, you may be tempted to drive anyway. Do yourself a favor and think about the long-term consequences before making the short-term or one-off decision. I get it. It's hard when you know you have gotten away with it before. But just because you got away with it before doesn't mean you will again. You are an easy target if the police know you, and those tickets get expensive. Use your personal commitment as a filter, and resist taking an easy way out instead of a long-term, greater achievement.

Goals and targets:

Here is a CHECKLIST to help you plan. I have added examples, and you can add other priorities and targets along with a date you'd like to complete them.

Item	Date
• *Public transportation—bus schedule* • *Bicycle (Human Society, Craigslist)* • *Valid license, if applicable* • ___________ • ___________ • ___________	• ___________ • ___________ • ___________ • ___________ • ___________ • ___________

*****

FOOD, CLOTHING, HYGIENE

As a returning citizen, you should automatically qualify for food stamps, depending on the state where you are incarcerated. Ask your release counselor or transition coordinator for help with accessing food stamps.

I am a strong supporter of using this resource for the first year you are out. If you can't afford food, you can't afford to stay alive, and nothing else matters. Having food stamps to subsidize your food budget for the first year gives you the opportunity to focus on building other areas on your checklist.

Research how much food costs per month. I probably spend somewhere between $200–$300 per month on food when I am being conservative. Knowing how you are going to shop for food will save you money and time.

Tip: *Start paying attention to how much it costs for you to eat once you get out. After you get a job and have a regular paycheck, I recommend setting aside the same amount of money from each check as the amount you are spending with food stamps.* For example, if you spend $200 a month purchasing food with your food stamps, make a goal to save $200/month of your income to create a habit of buying food. This has multiple benefits:

- You will create a habit of budgeting what you need for food.
- You will build an emergency savings fund. Take the $200/month example. After six months, you will have saved $1200!

*****

Not to state the obvious, but you are also going to want clothes to wear, especially ones that fit! Here is a simple checklist of clothes you will want to obtain:

- seven pairs of underwear
- seven pairs of socks
- five T-shirts
- two jeans
- two pants (slacks)
- two dress shirts
- one sweatshirt
- one coat (cold climate)
- one pair of tennis shoes
- one pair of dress shoes

This might seem like a long list, but you can get all of this at thrift stores for relatively cheap prices. Go for *new* when it comes to socks and underwear though for obvious reasons. I bet I could get all of this for $200.

Get creative; listen to some Macklemore and "Thrift Shop" to fill your closet with clean but inexpensive items to wear. If you stick to your personal commitment to change and work toward the life you want to live, you will have plenty of opportunities to buy and wear the clothes you want in the future. Remember, ***you are investing in your future by getting what you need now at a price you can afford.***

Many communities have organizations or churches that also help with clothing. Ask your counselor for a list of organizations, which provide resources in your community.

Many times, these same resources will also have toiletry supplies or at least be able to connect you with places that can provide some support. Don't be afraid to ask. Remember, this isn't the life you will always have. You are literally starting over. Everyone needs help every now and then. Ask for help now so you can help others later.

Goals and targets:

Here is a CHECKLIST to help you plan. I have added examples, and you can add other priorities and targets along with a date you'd like to complete them.

Item	Date
• *Food stamps*	• __________
• *Clothes checklist*	• __________
• *Food budge*	• __________
• *Hygiene budget*	• __________
• __________	• __________
• __________	• __________

*****

DOCUMENTATION

This is one of the most important categories of items on your checklist. Here are your top three *must-have* pieces of documentation:

- ID/license
- Social Security card
- Birth certificate

If you were not given an ID when you got out, you will have to go to the DMV. Just remember, you will likely need other forms of identification, like a birth certificate, in order to get your ID or license. You will also likely need to bring proof of living address. You can do this by bringing in an official piece of mail, like a utility bill, bank statement, or PO letter addressed to you and mailed to your current address.

I am sure there are different variations based on the state you live in, so I recommend asking your counselor about the process and what documentation the prison will provide you before you get out.

Here is an online resource to get important documents:

- *https://www.usa.gov/replace-vital-documents*

*****

Your local government agency, the Department of Human Services, can provide you with some guidance on the best way to secure documentation. This can be one of the most frustrating tasks on the checklist to accomplish because you might go several places just to find out you have to go somewhere else first.

If you start feeling overwhelmed, take a moment and breathe. There is a way to acquire everything you need; I promise. People do it all the time.

Tip: *This is a great opportunity to put your PO to work. They should be able to help you connect with the right organizations and ser-*

vices to get your documentation in order. And feel free to contact me with any questions.

GOALS AND TARGETS

Here is a CHECKLIST to help you plan. I have added examples, and you can add other priorities and targets along with a date you'd like to complete them.

Item	Date
• *State-issued ID/license* • *Social Security card* • *Birth certificate* • *Proof of address* • _______________ • _______________	• _______________ • _______________ • _______________ • _______________ • _______________ • _______________

*****

BANK ACCOUNT

Having a bank account is important for functioning as a productive community member. I realize many of us are more familiar with the cash-only lifestyle. But if you are going to follow through with your personal commitment to change, you are going to need a bank account.

Before you get a bank account, you definitely need an ID. You will normally need to have two forms of photo ID. Many times, banks will not accept prison IDs. Don't ask me why. It's absolutely ridiculous, but you may have to get creative.

If you don't have two pieces of ID for the bank to accept, ask your employer for a work ID. Many banks will accept work IDs. What does that mean? Well, if you have a job, you ask your boss to use a picture of you and create a photo ID that verifies you as an employee for your job. Seriously!

Most banks will not issue you a checking account until you have a savings account with them for a certain amount of time. I recommend reaching out to credit unions and community banks first since they usually don't charge fees. Many times, larger banks require a minimum amount of cash in your account at all times and sometimes charge fees.

Also, don't attempt to open an account without money. It is best to have at least $100 cash with you to open the account. In the meantime, you can utilize check cashing companies until you are able to open a bank account. These are good for temporary services but end up costing you money in the long run with fees.

Research the banks in your area by asking the following questions to find the one that fits your needs:

- Do they have a required minimum balance?
- Do they have fees?
- What type of first-time banking accounts do they offer?

Ideally, you will want to get to a place where you have both a checking account and a savings account.

*****

Make a personal financial plan

If you haven't done it yet, I recommend doing research about how to create a personal financial plan and budget. Make it a goal to always save a minimum of 10 percent of each paycheck in an account you keep for emergencies only. The goal is to build this account to reach six months of expenses. *Putting money IN isn't the hard part; NOT spending the money on nonemergencies is the HARD part.*

Work your food stamps plan I mentioned earlier. Use your savings account for this.

The more bills you can pay through your account online, the better. It can be easier to budget and track your expenses that go through your account versus spending cash.

Create a financial plan, and *make a personal commitment* to follow it until the plan becomes a habit. The plan should include an emergency fund: three to six months of expenses saved, set aside 10 percent of each paycheck in your savings, and find a way to gratefully offer 10 percent of your check to something you care about.

All financial experts I have studied mention the act of gifting in their financial plans. In the religious world, it can be called *tithing*. This is an important part of our reconnecting with the community and expressing our care.

Goals and targets:

Here is a CHECKLIST to help you plan. I have added examples, and you can add other priorities and targets along with a date you'd like to complete them.

Item	Date
• *Acquire state-issued ID/license* • *Have accepted proof of address (mail with your name addressed to you)* • *Acquire a second ID (i.e., employer identification, passport)* • *Research the best banking options available* • ___________________ • ___________________	• _______ • _______ • _______ • _______ • _______ • _______

*****

HEALTH CARE

The subject of health care is a frustrating topic for almost everyone in the United States. It's confusing, intimidating, uncomfortable, and downright terrible at times. Our health care opportunities change with our presidents and vary from state to state.

Currently, in Oregon, everyone who gets out of prison qualifies for the state health care plan. I do not know if that is the case with every state since the health care landscape is incredibly inefficient and inconsistent in our country.

If you take medication, it is very important for you to secure some type of health care. The Department of Human Services is going to be the main organization that facilitates your state's health insurance plans. If you are having trouble getting answers to your questions regarding health care, have someone look up this website and get the specific information you are looking for:

- *https://www.medicaid.gov/state-overviews/index.html*

There should be workers in your state called assisters whose job is to assist individuals with applying for health care insurance. Once you get out, you can look up "local health care assisters" to find support in this process.

Like the documentation task, this one is also a very difficult task to navigate. If you start to feel defeated or frustrated, take a moment and pause. Give yourself a break. Take a walk, or make a bagel. Dealing with health care and insurance will make even the squarest individual go postal.

Goals and targets:

Here is a CHECKLIST to help you plan. I have added examples, and you can add other priorities and targets along with a date you'd like to complete them.

Item	Date
• *Check-in with DHS*	• _________
• *Find a primary care provider*	• _________
• *Set up pharmacy account if need medication (Walgreens/ Rite Aid/Walmart)*	• _________
• *Find a dental provider (PNW Dental)*	• _________
• *Find a vision provider (if needed)*	• _________
• _________	• _________
• _________	• _________
• _________	• _________

*****

SUPPORT SYSTEM

Your network determines your net worth.
(Tim Sanders, author and speaker)

To achieve true freedom, you are going to need to develop a healthy support system in your community. This means you are going to have to find people who are not likely familiar with you. This can be very uncomfortable, but it is worth every bit to step out of your comfort zone and create a new social network of healthy individuals.

One of the most important people in your support system is going to be your mentor. Finding a mentor is a unique task for everyone. My *number one* rule for finding a mentor is to look for someone who has achieved something you want to achieve. From there, it is important to ask the ethical question: "Did they achieve it in a way I'd like to be remembered for?"

I have several mentors in my life, some whom I have never met but follow through their social media, books, and programs. Others are those I know personally and whom I meet with regularly. Not all my mentors are living exactly how I want, but all have achieved something I'd like to also achieve. When it comes to mentors, I am like a sponge; I soak up what I want to learn from them and squeeze out the rest.

Mentors are a great resource to bounce ideas off of, ask questions, and get guidance on decisions you may be unsure of making. A good mentor doesn't have to be an expert but a trusted individual who can direct you to expert resources. I have learned, it is most important to have a mentor for these important areas:

- *Finance*
- *Business/employment*
- *Physical health*
- *Relationship health*
- *Spiritual health*

These are five key categories in life, which can influence your freedom. When you meet someone who you learn is living a life in one or more of those areas, they may be someone who you want to ask to mentor you.

Finding a healthy personal mentor while you are still in prison can be extremely difficult, but what you can do is start writing down what you are looking for in a mentor:

- What do you want them to have achieved?
- What areas in life are they successful in?
- What skills would you like them to teach you?
- How available are they, or how frequently would you like to meet with them?
- How do you want them to hold you accountable?

The answers to these questions will help you identify someone as a potentially great mentor for you. Use the "Mentor Assessment Questions" worksheet in the "Resources" section to help you. And when you identify someone who meets your description, you will be ready to approach and ask them.

*****

How to ask for mentoring

You may have an opportunity to meet a mentor when you are still in prison, though it is rare. Some transitional organizations, like Sponsors Inc. in Eugene, Oregon, provide a mentor program that initiates contact *before* their clients are released.

No matter what, if you want to achieve a life of freedom, then you are going to have to ask some people to mentor you when you get out.

It can be awkward to ask someone to be your mentor, but I assure you, most people in a position of being a mentor are more than willing to offer some feedback. Like any relationship, the mentor-mentee relationship must be cultivated in trust.

I recommend asking a potential mentor if they would be willing to meet you for coffee. If they say yes, make an appointment, show up early, and be willing to pay for their coffee. This is a great way to show them you value their time. Their time is valuable, and they are doing you a huge service.

Be willing to pay for their time.

Your time is valuable too. Consider the coffee meeting an opportunity for you to find out about them, their life, and their experience to determine if they would be a good mentor for you. Not unlike an interview, you should ask questions related to what you'd like to learn from them. Once you determine you'd like to see them on a regular basis, it is your responsibility to make the first move.

When it comes to popping the question, be direct: *"Would you be interested in mentoring me on the subject of _______________?"*

If they agree (most will), set a scheduled time and place to meet on a regular basis. I suggest starting with twice a month.

As I referred to earlier, some re-entry organizations offer a mentoring program. If you are involved in one, please take advantage of the opportunity!

Finding a mentor

I have yet to hear a story of a returning citizen finding a top-shelf mentor at a bar. I'm sure the opportunity could happen, but I recommend looking at other places to find qualified mentors.

Where do the professionals connect?

You will find qualified mentors all over your community. If you attend a church or spiritual organization, you will likely find qualified mentors. There are likely community events put on by your local chamber of commerce or city club where many professionals and influencers connect. Fundraisers for nonprofits and ribbon-cutting events are also great places to meet potential mentors.

Take it from me, showing up to these events for the first time was one of the most intimidating things I ever went through. I was so nervous and felt more out of place than I ever had before. And to make it worse, once I broke the ice and started talking to people, I found out how smart, experienced, and educated these people were, which made me even more uncomfortable!

But I didn't succumb to my fear of being uncomfortable and found myself learning and being mentored by the very people I originally felt uncomfortable being around.

If you are nervous about networking (like almost everyone is), check out an article I wrote on LinkedIn in which I share ideas that have helped me network much more effectively. I have included this article just after the GOALS AND TARGETS checklist.

*****

GOALS AND TARGETS

Here is a CHECKLIST to help you plan. I have added examples, and you can add other priorities and targets along with a date you'd like to complete them.

Item	Date
• *Create a support system plan* • *Complete mentor assessment* • *Research community organizations offering mentor programs* • *Get a schedule of NA/AA meetings* • ___________ • ___________	• ___________ • ___________ • ___________ • ___________ • ___________ • ___________

*****

Five tips and five questions to network successfully

"Your network determines your net worth." "A man is not an island." "It's not what you know, it's who you know."

We have all heard these quotes, and many of us have said them. These are sayings that reinforce the importance of networking.

Investopedia defines networking as "<u>the exchange of information and ideas among people with a common profession or special interest, usually in an informal social setting</u>." Networking is universally important to everyone.

Traditionally, we associate networking with business. However, *life is about relationships*—relationships with our family, friends, coworkers, relationships as customers, with strangers, and the person at the desk, telling me my plane is delayed.

Relationships are everywhere. They are the lifeblood of the *network* we call community, economy, culture, and our lives.

Think about it: Who do you know? How do you relate or interact with them? And what comes out of those relationships?

We have all seen the movie scene where the cool guy walks into the lounge with the pretty girl on his arm. The man at the door opens it for them and says, "Good evening, Mr. _______," and gets a bill slipped into their pocket. Who hasn't imagined that experience?

Here's the great news: Anyone can have that experience, and so much more, simply through effectively *networking* in your community.

"NETWORKING? But I HATE networking!"

"I am not good at talking to strangers." "I don't know how I'd be able to relate." "I don't feel comfortable talking about myself." "I'm an introvert."

Don't worry. It doesn't matter if you are an introvert. It doesn't matter if you feel uncomfortable talking to strangers. It doesn't matter if you feel like you can't relate. Why? Because networking is not about you.

THE FIRST RULE OF NETWORKING IS, IT'S NOT ABOUT YOU, IT'S ABOUT OTHERS.

Effective networking is learning about others. That's it! That's all you need to know!

If all you learn from this article is *"networking is not about you, it's about others"* and how to apply it, you will *build an incredible network of relationships, increase your sales, find yourself involved in opportunities you never imagined*, and so much more.

You will also be miles ahead of the majority of business professionals who spend copious amounts of hours and money at networking events.

My network will tell you, one of the greatest skills I have is *connecting people who will work well together.* When someone is speaking to me about a problem or project they have, I seem to be able to know someone who might be able to help. Currently, I utilize this skill when pairing clients of our nonprofit, <u>Changing Patterns</u>, with mentors.

Early in my professional career, I focused my attention on working with struggling businesses and start-ups. One of my greatest networking connections happened when I was working with a business that was on a five-year annual revenue decline.

I was working with "old dogs who didn't want to learn new tricks." They were stubborn, beat up from the recession, and had goals like, "just survive the quarter and pay the bills."

I tried to change their systems, but they weren't ready to change their habits. I tried to increase sales, but they didn't want to make cold calls. I tried to motivate the staff to think differently, but I was the "new guy on the block" without experience.

In the end, I took responsibility for creating sales (THE most important part of doing business) and took to the streets, cold-calling.

I made a few sales here and there, but I kept running into a problem: *the name of one of our direct competitors* (not the company itself but the name of a person in that company).

After being told "no" hundreds of times because of this name that kept coming up, I had to find out who this character was, so I walked into their business to meet the man behind the name.

When I walked into the building and met this individual, instead of telling them about me, I asked them about them. You follow? I listened to what they said and learned information that became instrumental to the success of the company I worked with at the time.

I *listened* and learned he was unhappy. I *listened* and learned he was looking for a new opportunity. I *listened* and learned what his endgame was, what his goals were in life, and where he wanted to be in twenty years.

Did you catch that?

Within one year from the day I walked into that company, the unhappy owner walked away from an unhealthy work environment and partnered with my struggling client. Since then, my client has grown its customer base and revenue dramatically so much, so they don't need me anymore.

Oh, and the unhappy man who established such a loyal customer base is now a happy, driven, and prosperous partner working in a growing company and providing more freedom to its owners and employees.

All thanks to effective networking.

This stuff works, and it is not nearly as threatening as you may think. *Great networking is focused on learning about the other person.* You don't have to be an expert salesperson or social butterfly. All you have to do is be interested in other people.

Here are *five tips* and *five questions* you can use to help guide you in your networking experience, which will *lead you to more opportunities, help you accomplish your goals, and build some of the greatest relationships you will ever have.*

Tip #1: Network with the intent to learn

As I wrote earlier, effective networking is learning about the other person. The FIRST RULE OF NETWORKING: *It's not about you, it's about THEM.*

How many times have you been in a conversation with someone and all they are doing is talk about themselves or try to get something from you? It sucks.

I have some heartbreaking news for you: Most people AREN'T actually that interested in you.

This sounds harsh, but this is a reality.

People have their own lives. They are stressed about bills, relationships, kids, and work. They are thinking about what they need to pick up at the store or why their boss said what they said. They are remembering they have things to do. Most people don't have the time or energy, and many don't even have the desire to think about you.

Take a moment. Take a deep breath. Accept the harsh news. Now read on.

Guess what, this is GREAT news for you. Why? *Because effective networking is not about you*, IT'S ABOUT THEM!

Going into a conversation with the *intent to learn about the other person* takes off the pressure to perform.

Introverts, I can hear you cheering! You don't have to talk about yourselves. In fact, you shouldn't even talk about yourself unless someone asks.

Don't get too relaxed. To be a great networker and build strong relationships, you are going to have to *take the initiative.*

Tip #2: Start the conversation.

Don't wait for someone to approach you. Those who wait stay hungry. Those who initiate get fed and *get to feed others*. You are 100 percent responsible for getting the job done.

If you are nervous about introducing yourself to a stranger or starting a conversation, you are not alone. Check it out, <u>Inc. magazine</u> did a study, which found *69 percent of LEADERS* are scared to talk to their own employees! These are employees they likely know!

One could only imagine how many more people are actually scared to talk to a stranger!

So relax. You are not alone. Almost everyone gets nervous talking to a stranger. And most likely, the person you initiate a conversation with is also scared to talk to you. Trust me, they will be relieved when YOU start the conversation.

I am *always* uncomfortable initiating a conversation with someone I don't know, and I do it every day! Before I meet someone new, my mind is thinking, *What am I going to say? How will I be able to find something to relate to them? What if they don't like me? What if I say something stupid?*

Don't worry. I will give you five questions you can use so you don't ever have to worry about what you are going to say at any networking event.

And remember, you don't need to worry about whether or not they are going to like you because *effective networking is not about you, it's about them.*

Tip # 3: Remember their name.

Dale Carnegie's *How to Win Friends and Influence People* talks at length about the importance of remembering someone's name. Saying someone's name is so personal and captures immediate attention. Think about when someone says your name. You immediately turn your attention to them.

Remembering someone's name builds connection and trust. Networking is about building relationships. Relationships are built on trust. Trust comes after credibility is established. Credibility is established through likability. *People like it when others remember their names.* Follow?

When I meet someone new, I *make it a point to say their name three to four times in the first few minutes of the conversation.* <u>Repetition engraves the person's name in your memory</u>. Doing this will significantly reduce the number of times you will embarrassingly have to ask, "I'm sorry, what was your name again?"

Build trust through the small effort of remembering someone's name.

"What is your name?" This is the first question you should ask someone who you don't know.

Tip #4: Ask questions.

Curiosity might have killed the cat, but it has attributed to some of my greatest accomplishments, experiences, and financial achievements.

Be curious. ASK QUESTIONS. And of course, listen.

Asking questions gives others an opportunity to share with you about who they are, what they do, and how you can relate.

Think of all the great interviewers on TV, podcasts, radio, and in magazine articles. Where does it start? It starts with a question.

The key is asking the right questions based on the situation. Networking opportunities happen all the time in many different situations.

Ask questions with the intent to learn because you WANT to build a relationship with this person and engage in a fulfilling conversation.

I will give you questions you can ask, which will influence impactful conversation where likability, credibility, and trust will be the result.

Approach the connection with the intent to learn, start the conversation, remember their name (ask for it first), ask questions, and then LISTEN.

Tip #5: LISTEN

It is sad but true; people have to be reminded to listen. Good communication happens when one party receives the correct (context) message from the one delivering. Otherwise, it's just noise.

When my extended family gets together around a table, an outsider watching would wonder who everyone is talking TO because

EVERYONE is talking, and no one seems to be listening. Many times, this is what networking events are like. Everyone is racing to tell as many people about whatever service or product they have to offer.

Be different. Listen. Remember. LEARN about them.

When we go into a conversation with the intent to learn, we stop thinking about ourselves and become listeners. Being a great listener is one of the most memorable and attractive traits in people. Think about someone in your life who is a great listener. How do you feel about them?

In this day and age where everyone is pounding their opinions on all communication outlets, the listener is rare.

Rare equates to valuable. A valuable person can build a network with a NET WORTH!

For the introvert or the person who is worried about saying something stupid, not being liked, or not knowing how to relate to others, going into a conversation with the intent to learn takes attention off you. So relax. Just *listen* and *learn.*

The easiest way to be an effective listener is to have some killer questions in your conversational tool belt available at a moment's notice. Use these questions, not like an interview but to relate and have a fulfilling conversation.

SECTION 3

Navigating Technology

I fall behind on everything else when I try to keep up with technology. That statement is the truest way I can describe my experience with technology since I got out.

Let me alleviate a concern you may have regarding the challenge of understanding technology: *The minute you start to think you understand any part of technology, something new comes out.* Don't stress, few people actually know what is really going on with technological evolution. If you are one of them, like my boy, Roper, then this next section might be more of a review. If you are like me, then dig in and learn everything you can from this next section. These lessons will save you from experiencing the many growing pains I had to deal with.

When I went to prison, we had flip phones. My friend had just purchased the first iPhone with the lighter app where you could flick the screen, and the lighter would light up. I don't even remember holding the phone, just briefly seeing it, and then I went to prison. That was January 2010.

When I got out, I was handed an iPhone 6s and given an opportunity to fix phones—fix phones! I went from stealing music on LimeWire to having access to the entire globe through a rectangle in my pocket. And *if* you understand the last sentence, then you are leaps ahead of many people getting out of prison.

Look, my first few weeks, I was lost with these handheld computers we now call phones. Every time I pushed a button, I thought I broke it! After a few days, you won't be intimidated by the phones for long; you'll be hooked. And if you are like my friend, Roper, excited to try out all this technology after being gone for ten years, then welcome to your sandbox. There are all sorts of exciting things to discover!

Not only is the hardware different (smaller and more accessible), the software, "apps" (short for applications), are an entirely new subject to learn! Even the internet has changed from how we used it before to how we use it now. By the time you are reading this, the Internet may have changed again, and our entire communication platforms may be completely different again. *Technology moves fast!*

In this section, I am going to share with you some common technology tools, how to use them, and offer some etiquette suggestions regarding social media and what to expect. These phones are a blast and one of the greatest things man has created. Like any great creation, it comes with great responsibility. Learn how to use this tool effectively, and your level of freedom can be unimaginable!

*****

THE BIG THREE

Almost everything you do online will eventually ask for your email, to create a password, and verify yourself with a phone number.

Before you get going into the world of the Internet, make sure you have set up your online *big three.*

- *Email*—first/last name combination preferred
- *Password*—create a password system; this is a system of passwords you use that you can easily remember.
- *Phone number verification*—this is where they send a code to your phone or email to verify you are a real human; this happens because of people running scams or a program

called a *bot* developed to create false accounts and steal your information.

Note that some apps require you to set up and log on to your account on the computer before you can use them on your phone.

When it comes to your password system, create one you will remember. You will have to change passwords somewhat frequently, so having a system you remember will help you. Example: Use one version of a password for social media and email and a different one for finance-related log-ons, like the app for my bank or credit cards or Credit Karma.

Use a combination of letters, numbers, and characters (&$#%@*!) with every password. *A good practice is changing the most important ones every six months.*

It's okay to save your password for some apps, but I don't recommend saving your passwords for your financial log-ons.

Use the fingerprint option to log on from your phone. And a note for conspiracy theorists: *They already have your fingerprints.*

*****

LIFE ONLINE

What you need to know about life and the internet is ON the internet. If you have been locked up for quite a few years, then you are in for a whole new way of life. The internet is our encyclopedia, our communication tool, our office, and our sales force. The internet is a utility embedded in our culture.

If you have fears about being online, being tracked, being listened to, and having your information looked at, then you are normal. I'd like to alleviate any fears you may have about this by letting you know that *they are listening.* Any information you type into or say around your phone may be saved and sold to the highest bidder so they can influence you.

Before you wrap your dome in tinfoil and run to the woods, it's important for you to know that the majority of your information is sold as marketing material to companies who want to sell you something.

But, YES, everything you do on the internet and around your phone is tracked. If anyone tells you otherwise, they are either purposefully lying to you or completely naive to the truth of the matter.

During my re-entry journey, I have had the privilege of working for a company that gave me access to high-tech analytics software which put me in the room with some of the brightest tech geniuses. I have attended conferences where the leaders in digital marketing told me what is happening online, how they are getting your data, what is being tracked, and how they use it to get you to buy stuff.

It's happening! I tell you this, not to create fear but to inform you. This information is to help you decide, with awareness, how much you are willing to expose.

*****

COMPUTERS AND INTERNET

The Apple community is very confident that their computers cannot get viruses. The PC loyalists will argue that their own version of security measures is top-shelf. After all my research, at this juncture, choosing a brand is a matter of personal preference. Whatever system you choose, here are a few good habits to keep your information safe:

- *If it looks "phishy," it probably is.* Phishing is a term for *"the fraudulent practice of sending emails purporting to be from reputable companies in order to induce individuals to reveal personal information, such as passwords and credit card numbers."* These emails can look very official, but check with the company over the phone if you notice something "phishy."

- *Keep your banking info to yourself.* Banking online is a common practice. However, never save your bank or other financial passwords on your computer or especially on your internet browser. Memorize them.

- *Change passwords.* I probably change my passwords twice a year or if I make a mistake and something hacks me. Articles recommend changing your passwords every sixty to ninety days. You decide how frequent, but you will want to change them from time to time.
- *Consider monitoring companies.* If you would like more information about monitoring companies when you get out, email your questions to info@changingpatternsinc.org with "online monitoring" in the subject line.

*****

PHONES

Similar to computers, phones are a preferential experience. I personally love the iPhone, and I have friends who wouldn't think of leaving their Android. Generally, the term *Android* refers to phones that are NOT an iPhone.

Our phones have become an extension of ourselves. They are extremely addicting. I thought I would never be like those crazy people sitting around a table, looking at their phones. I was wrong. I can be caught breaking good phone etiquette from time to time.

There is some phone etiquette that, when applied, will set you apart from the norm. Phone etiquette may not always go noticed, but you'll appreciate it when someone gives you the same respect.

Put your phone away when you are in a meeting or sharing a meal. Don't look at your phone. Don't answer it. Don't check your Facebook likes. Seriously, everyone does it. I do it. It's rude. It's obnoxious. It's the worst.

Driving and texting is super dangerous and illegal. This is the easiest thing to do, and it is the quickest way to find yourself in jail if you hit someone, and they realize you were on your phone. Get a magnet to hold your phone up so you can listen to music or follow directions, but avoid texting and driving at all costs.

Put the phone away an hour before bed. If you keep looking at your phone, you are going to keep looking at your phone. They won't go away on their own; you have to put your phone down. There are many studies on how the light from phones (or screens in general) negatively affects our sleep, not to mention your eyesight when looking at your phone in the dark. I recommend making it a habit to put away your phone at least an hour before bed. Trust me, you'll appreciate the break eventually.

Don't start your day by looking at your phone. Everyone does! The first thing we do in the morning is check our phones. It's killing our souls, I'm sure. Get up. Enjoy some coffee. Read a book. Workout. Do your best to keep your healthy morning routine for as long as you can. Also, looking at your phone first thing in the morning is not healthy for your eyesight.

*****

SOCIAL MEDIA

Social media is one of the greatest and worst technological advancements in our history. Social media has given us the opportunity to connect with everyone in the world. The benefits are incredible. The drawbacks can be detrimental.

Personally, I love social media as a tool that I can use to create incredible opportunities for myself and others. However, like any tool, when misused, it can cause serious damage. Legendary motivator and business mogul, Grant Cardone, has stated that *there are three types of people when it comes to social media:*

1. People who don't use it
2. People who are USED BY it
3. People who use it

Most people live in the second category, spending most of their time scrolling through the platforms, staring at pictures, and reading the opinions of others while spouting off their own unsolicited opinions. I wish I could say I have refrained from attending the second category, but I have my moments where I am brutally used by social media. These are "empty calories."

The third category is those who have figured out how to use social media to improve their *real life* through means of making a difference, creating income, or building an effective network that influences change.

This third category is where I recommend you strive to be part of on a regular basis.

*****

SOCIAL ETIQUETTE

The world is an offensive place these days. People have more platforms than ever from which to speak their opinion. This has created a lot of noise in the world, which can be overwhelming and disappointing. If you want to be effective at building a solid network and using social media as a tool, you will want to consider some of these suggestions:

EVERYONE *can see you, and it's on there forever.* Businesses look at social media to help determine who to hire. Your boss will follow you. Your PO is on there. What you post goes out into the social world, and many times it has repercussions later in the future. Think of all the celebrities getting canceled for things they posted years ago. And if you think deleting things is the answer, think again. There are huge databases that keep ALL data, deleted or otherwise, just in case. Just be aware, convictions *can be* and *have been* accomplished with social media content.

Don't air out your relationship problems. More than enough people spend much of their energy complaining about their relationships on social media. This cannot help their relationships at all. It's best to keep relationship complaints private to the relationship and your support group. Keep it off the Internet!

Not everyone is your friend. There are plenty of scammers and hacks going on in social media. If you are receiving duplicate friend requests from someone, reach out to them on their original account to see if they sent you the request to connect. This is mainly an issue on Facebook. Either way, message people first. Personally, I don't normally accept friend duplicates anymore. Two reasons: (1) it could be a hack, or (2) they are screwing up and making new accounts to avoid trouble.

Either way, I don't want any part of it.

Attachments and chain letters are bad luck. People are going to send you how much they love you in all sorts of fun ways. Chain letters are going to come through your messenger. Play at your own risk. Many of these attachments have ways for people to hack your account.

Don't take it personally. People have gotten much more confident with the way they talk to each other online. There is much less of a threat with a screen between them and other people. If you find yourself getting angry at people online, you probably ought to limit your social media exposure. What we understand as *respect* in prison is not the same philosophy or way of life out here. If you want to stay out, then you will have to figure out ways to ignore or use social skills on disrespectful people, online and in person.

Headlines and news aren't always true. Fake news is an epidemic. Headline announcements are regarded as concrete facts. Do yourself a favor and research before buying in on a headline or reposting something online.

Play. Learn. Figure it out. Your social media pages are part of your online real estate. Experiment and learn the landscape. Eventually, you are going to have an idea or a message you are going to want to share with the public. This is your platform, and it is best to learn some of them enough to be effective. They change in popularity frequently, so don't feel pressured to learn them all. Learn the big ones, and practice until you like your part in the system.

Keeping up with the Jones. Recent studies have suggested that social media may be responsible for an increase in depression and anxiety. Social media can bring on the curse of comparing oneself to others. It can be easy to look at the success posted by others and think you aren't getting things accomplished fast enough or that you are failing. Please remember these things:

- What people post on social media is almost never the full story. Most posts are highlights and many exaggerate to create attention.
- Life is not a competition; it is a journey unique to all. Avoid comparing yourself to others so you are able to truly enjoy your own journey.
- Be smart and treat social media as if it is real life, and at the very least, you won't compromise your own personal beliefs. Be your own best friend. Don't make life harder on yourself. Make it fun and easy.
- Use social media as a tool to connect with people, share ideas, debate, and create opportunities.

*****

SUMMARY

Whether you served a short sentence and are just catching up with tech or you are entering this technological world for the first time, it is important to your sanity and safety to learn how to USE technology rather than being used by it.

Many of us are susceptible to the addictive characteristics of this tool and can become used by it, just like drugs and alcohol have done to our lives.

Please be aware of the power and influence of technology, social media, and all that is available. Late nights watching videos or talking to bots mimicking people will create low productive mornings. Utilizing the ability to provide a captive audience, a product, or a service can create high-volume bank accounts.

Don't be a tool. Use it as a tool.

Navigating Obstacles and Barriers

It's normal to have fears about returning to society. *Will I be able to find a place to live? Will someone hire me? What are people going to think when they find out I was in prison? Are they going to turn me away because of my past? Will I fit in?*

The process of returning back to the community is going to have obstacles and barriers that *you* need to navigate and overcome. Accomplishing this requires you to dig up that *personal commitment to change* and have *the willingness to do whatever it takes* to overcome each barrier and obstacle to become free. Some of these barriers are unfair, unjust, and downright mean. However, it is *your responsibility* to overcome them.

Imagine you are on a pilgrimage or quest. Your quest has a mission to *successfully complete parole and create the life you want.* There are goals you need to accomplish on your quest. You must

- find employment,
- secure a safe place to live,
- develop prosocial hobbies and relationships, and
- build financial prosperity.

You must be prepared when embarking on any quest. All heroes in epic stories start out with packs of supplies, maps, tools, and some type of guide to help them achieve their mission. This *survival guide* is part of your tool kit in this quest. Continue to use it to prepare for the obstacles that may come your way. The following section is meant to prepare and inform you about situations that could happen, which are not easy to handle. I write about this as bluntly as possible because overcoming these barriers and obstacles is not a smooth experience. Use this section to learn ways to cope with, navigate through, and overcome these obstacles and barriers most returning citizens can expect.

*****

OVERCOMING REJECTION

Human beings naturally fear rejection. I don't believe anyone actually *enjoys* being rejected, and I know none of us enjoy being rejected because of our past. Being rejected because of your past is a common obstacle you will face as you reenter the community.

The main types of rejection we encounter are related to housing options and potential employment opportunities. Even though we can expect this to happen, it still doesn't feel good. It is extremely discouraging to be told "NO" repeatedly.

Be persistent. When you are looking for employment or a place to live, it is important to remain persistent. These are the consequences we never considered before we committed our crimes. Because we made those past decisions, we have to work harder than others to find employment and especially housing opportunities.

If you have a mentor, utilize them as a resource to connect you to those who may be able to help and someone to talk to when you are feeling discouraged. A good mentor is going to listen to you when you are feeling defeated and give you encouragement to push forward on your quest until you are successful.

After sharing your feelings with your mentor, get back out there and push yourself. Sometimes it takes much longer than you anticipated to be successful, but *the only ones who fail are those who give up*. Just because things aren't working out exactly how you planned doesn't mean they are failing. It just means things are different than expected, and sometimes you need to adapt to changes in order to accomplish what you are looking for.

Remember your goals, your endgame, your personal commitment, and what freedom looks like to you. Keep them at the forefront of your mind while you battle rejection because they can be like fuel to motivate you when you need them.

Another rejection that could happen is in personal relationships. In my experience, it is pretty disappointing when I've formed a new relationship with someone, and later, they decide to end it because of my past. This isn't as common as you might think, but it does happen.

I have learned to be open about my past early in every new relationship. Some may disagree with my openness, but I have found a real sense of freedom comes with being open about having a criminal past. Whether it's a job opportunity, new friends, or a date, I usually reveal my past as soon as possible. This gives the other party an opportunity to choose before becoming emotionally invested.

Not everyone is ready to give people second chances or wants to affiliate with someone with a criminal past. You know what? That's okay. I believe everyone should have the freedom to decide who they want and don't want in their life. As people who desire freedom, we should respect their freedom to choose and to be able to make informed choices.

I have found those who decided not to be in a relationship with me because of my past don't last very long in my mind or memory. You will likely forget them quicker than you met them. There are plenty of people in the world who will interest you, and they with you. I don't recommend investing much time in someone who has no interest in you.

Handling rejection is hard. When you are feeling discouraged, utilize your support network and trusted mentors as a place to share how you are feeling. Yes, it feels uncomfortable, but doing *healthy* things we are uncomfortable with offers us opportunities to grow.

Journaling is also a great tool to help you get your thoughts and feelings organized and understood. Journaling traps your thoughts and feelings on paper, so you are able to shake the burden a bit and evaluate how to move forward. Many ideas and solutions to problems were discovered when frustrated people journaled about their problems.

Rejection is part of life. You must learn how to handle rejection, cope with the feelings that come with rejection, and develop the skill to overcome them.

One way to overcome rejection is to immerse yourself in it. If you want to test yourself and build your tolerance to objections, then I suggest getting a job as a cold-calling sales executive. It will help you develop your communication skills, find great money-making opportunities, and get over any fear of rejection.

Spending a few years in sales taught me valuable communication skills, insight into people, and how to overcome rejections. You can also find many coaches, motivational speakers, and gurus online who offer courses, seminars, and mentoring online and through books, which can help overcome rejection.

*****

HANDLING CONFLICT

In prison, conflicts are handled much like out in society. The only difference is handling a conflict with violence in society has a much worse consequence than in prison. A few months in the hole is nothing compared to getting sent back to prison for a fight. Handling a conflict with violence should be avoided at all costs because it's only going to *cost* you in the end.

Prison can help one develop the social skill of talking through a conflict. Unlike in the movies, most people in prison don't want things to escalate to violence. Violence disrupts the routine, which is uncomfortable. Learning to diffuse situations through communication in a violent atmosphere is a transferable skill that has incredible influence out here in society. You may have already developed this skill!

Think about a time when you faced a conflict with someone who was likely to resort to violence and was able to walk away unscathed. How were you able to stay calm in the face of danger? What did you say to defuse the situation? How did you close the situation so both of you walked away without facing the consequences of a fight or worse?

If you were able to navigate a situation like that in prison, nothing will ever come close to that level of threat with "normal" people out here. They aren't likely going to jump you or send a "torpedo." You can handle it.

When you find yourself in an argument or disagreement, try to just sit in the uncomfortable feeling and maintain control with your words. Most conflicts are caused by some type of miscommunication. One party did not get all the facts or made an assumption. Many times, in the height of emotion, someone just needs to be heard. If we listen, then we can hear what is causing the conflict. Listening with the intent to understand THEM gives us clues to be able to effectively resolve the conflict.

One of my favorite books that has helped me in this area is *Never Split the Difference* by Chris Voss. If you haven't read it yet, I highly suggest it.

*****

SAYING NO

When Warren Buffett, the richest man in the world, was asked about the "secret to his success," he replied, "For every one hundred *good* ideas that come across my desk, I say 'no' to ninety-nine of them."

There is a sense of freedom one gains when one learns the skill of saying no. Really, it's a skill to discern when to say no and when to say yes. There were many great ideas, which perished from distractions because someone was unable to say no.

Saying no to doing drugs, getting involved in a crime, or breaking your parole might seem like an easy feat right now. Prison is fresh in your mind still, and there's hope for a new life. And if it is difficult saying no to those things right now, then you have something to practice on.

Agreeing to requests that do not align with your personal commitment to change is a constant detriment to returning citizens' success in rejoining the community. Our loyalty to our past has brought us pain and is likely the cause of most of our incarceration. This is why developing the skill to say no at the right times is imperative for your success in achieving freedom.

This skill is developed through practice and a strong commitment to your personal change. In practice, you will build confidence, and your mistakes will offer lessons to reinforce "no" in the future.

Saying no has been one of the hardest things I have had to learn and something I continue to work on. I feel bad when I tell people no, and I have an insecurity about missing out on an opportunity. However, not every opportunity is a healthy one.

Imagine this scenario: It's late at night. Someone calls you for a ride across town because they need to get somewhere. You want to be a good friend, so you give them a ride. You get pulled over. You are both on parole, so they search the vehicle and find drugs on your friend. Now you are both in trouble. Scenarios like this are common for returning citizens.

In these big decision moments, your desire for a new life needs to be more important than being that person who says yes.

Saying no to the wrong things is a skill that is dependent on your commitment to your personal change. You will have to lean on your commitment to yourself and your future to carry you through these times.

You have to be your own best friend because no one is going to be a better friend to you than you will be to yourself. It's your choice to decide if your future and the lives you can positively affect are more important than the risk of saying yes to something potentially detrimental to you and your future.

Building a strong, healthy network is key to supporting your ability to say no. Your healthy network will support your decisions and balance any feelings of loneliness that come with saying no to others.

If someone asks you to do something that contradicts your personal commitment to change, ask yourself, "Will this help me or hurt me?" If it will hurt you, or if you are not sure it will help, then no is the right answer. If you are having a hard time responding with a hard no, say something like, "I am not available right now," or "I am not able to help you out." Eventually, you will need to learn to give a firm and assertive no to establish true boundaries. Until then, "I am busy" will suffice.

With all decisions, the results will support the action. I have found that each time I make the right decision, the result reinforces to me that the habit is healthy. Making the right decision for yourself will eventually lead to the results you are looking for in your life. The more good choices you make, the stronger the habit will be and the easier it is to make similar future decisions. The first ones are always the hardest, but none of them are easy.

If you said yes, and at some point, you realize the decision was not in your best interest, remember, *you can always change your mind.* There is no such thing as backing out when it comes to your life! *You have* the *choice to make a choice.* You may have to tactfully remove yourself from a situation, but please remember, you have the right to choose to change your mind and alter your decision and your future for the better. Exercise that right. Be your own best friend.

Remember, every time you say yes to something, you are saying no to something else. Make sure your yeses don't keep you away from freedom.

*****

POs AND MISCOMMUNICATION

Many people I have worked with have complained about frustrations with their PO and the system. I've heard it all from poor scheduling, lack of communication between organizations, and an unwillingness to provide the best support. There are many things broken in our criminal justice system, and the parole/post-prison supervision part has many faults.

As much as it sucks, early on, we are subject to authority figures running our lives. When you get out, these authority figures include your PO and treatment counselors. It is your job to do your best to fulfill the obligations put on you and communicate effectively when there are conflicts between those obligations.

You may encounter times when you are scheduled to see your PO and be at a treatment class at the same time. Or your PO might not be flexible with scheduling around your new job. This is incredibly frustrating!

Be proactive! If you see that a PO visit conflicts with a treatment class, it is YOUR RESPONSIBILITY to bring that conflict to everyone's attention. Don't project your anger, even if you feel angry. Use your communication skills and inform them as soon as possible that you are not going to be able to make one of the appointments. Don't be lazy with your communication. Pick up the phone and call. It sucks at the moment, but a proactive phone call is much easier to deal with than an upset PO or counselor.

POs and treatment providers don't always communicate effectively with each other. If you don't let them know, and there is an issue, then they are going to hold you responsible.

In prison, we are taught to be dependent on the schedule they provide. This is not the case once you get out. This is your life, even though sometimes it doesn't feel like it. You will be held accountable for missing an appointment, so take responsibility for conflicting appointments and inform ALL the parties as early as possible.

If you are having trouble with transportation, then let your PO know. Their job is to support your transition back to the community. Yes, their job is to hold you accountable to be a productive community member, but *they are also supposed to help you be successful too.* Utilize them as a resource and ask them to help you. Let your PO know, "I want to make it to my appointments on time. Are there any transportation resources I can access so I don't miss these appointments that are required of me?"

Supporting your success is part of their job description. Hold them accountable to this just as they hold you accountable to living as a prosocial community member.

*****

FINDING POSITIVE TIME FILLERS

You have to find healthy hobbies and leisure activities! I guarantee you will not want to spend every day bouncing from work to PO to class to sleep without having some sort of self-care activity that makes you smile. You have to have a reason to get up in the morning. And usually, in the early days of getting out of prison, work, PO, and class are not that satisfying.

What did you enjoy while you were in prison? Working out? Softball? Drawing? Basketball? Playing guitar? Pickleball? Before prison, did you have any healthy activities you enjoyed? Hiking? Swimming? Snow activities?

You can utilize social media, like Facebook, to find clubs or organizations that may offer events, gatherings, or locations where you can find these activities offered. Also, search "sports or activities near me" on Google for ideas.

It takes courage to walk into a place alone, but what you may find is a group of people who may become a healthy network. If you have a mentor or support group, this would be a great topic to bring up with them. Ask them what they like to do for fun. Maybe they could introduce you to something that fits with what you enjoy. You can also ask your PO, the people in your classes, or those you work with where you could find opportunities for activities.

Find something healthy to fill your time because the old adage is as true today as it was when it first was spoken: *"Idle hands are the devil's playthings."*

Be a friend to yourself, and find a hobby. Treat yourself to something leisurely to help you unwind, and enjoy the life you get to live!

Creditable Reputation

Credit balances criminal record

Your criminal record is one of the biggest barriers you will have to constantly overcome. This barrier shows up during many of life's big decision-making moments, like when you begin new relationships, apply for jobs, and attempt to rent a home.

One of the best equalizers to the debt your criminal record put you in is your credit score. Your credit score is the most powerful counterweight to your past criminal history IF (and that is a BIG "IF") you *build a healthy credit score.* If you fail to do so, your bad credit score only reinforces that your criminal record is a valid indication of who you are and your reputation!

I know this from very personal experience. As I write this, I am in transition, looking for a new place to live and struggling to find a place because I failed to maintain my credit responsibly. A few years prior, I invested in some business decisions, which I failed in because I wanted to "play" more than work. The "play" cost more than the income my business was bringing in, so I used credit cards as money available to spend. The result was a sizable debt beyond what I could maintain.

Eventually, I had to make a decision on what to pay off and what to let default because I did not make the income to support my past spending on credit. In the end, I defaulted on some credit cards and watched my incredible credit score plummet to a number not even high-interest loan offices considered.

The lessons I've learned are *painful* and unnecessary to someone willing to learn principles and have the discipline to apply them.

Look, it is tough to resist the urge to buy things you don't need or take the family and friends out when you get a new credit card. However, developing a habit of using your credit wisely will offer much greater opportunities to purchase *exciting* items and take your family on a dream vacation instead of a night in the bar.

WHAT IS CREDIT?

Webster defines *credit* as *"the ability of a customer to obtain goods or services before payment, based on the trust that payment will be made in the future; the quality of being believed or credited; favorable estimation; good reputation."*

Your credit score is what professionals, lenders, business, and property managers use to *determine if you have a good reputation and are of the quality to be trusted.*

We have to earn the trust back from the community as returning citizens. Our reputation is on thin ice when we first get out. But I have good news! TRUST CAN BE EARNED.

People want to believe in you! They want to cheer for you.

They want to be part of your comeback story! They want to trust you. All you have to do is give them a reason. How do you give them reasons to trust you?

- *Don't commit a crime.*
- *Be friendly.*
- *Learn how the community has agreed to speak to each other, and do it better (be friendly).*
- *Tell the truth, but don't be mean.*
- *Learn how to control yourself when you are angry.*
- *Help others.*
- *Be honest about yourself, but learn to tactfully communicate your history to others.*

- *Pay your bills.*
- *Behave prosocially, and make decisions that benefit others and the community as a whole (this includes benefiting yourself),*
- *Arrive a little early. Ten minutes early is "on time" when going to your job, meeting, interview, dinner with the family, date, and business transactions.*

These are just some examples of how to start building trust. Once you have the community's trust and a reputable credit score, there isn't much that can hold you back.

Building your financial credit reputation is actually not complicated. However, raising your credit score and maintaining high levels takes strong discipline to create this most important habit.

*****

BUILDING CREDIT TO MONITOR

On a computer, create your Credit Karma account. You will need an email address and your Social Security number. (Don't worry, Credit Karma is a trusted account.)

Download the Credit Karma app on your phone and log on. I suggest using the fingerprint option once you have it set up to avoid having to put in your password every time.

Look at your credit score and accounts that are found.

Most negative items should automatically fall off your *credit* reports **seven years** from the date of your first missed payment, at which point, your *credit* scores may start rising. But if you are otherwise using *credit* responsibly, your score may rebound to its starting point within three months to six *years* (per bankrate.com).

Credit Karma will suggest credit cards you will likely be approved to get. Apply for cards that don't charge interest if you pay them off the same month you use them.

Don't worry about getting dinged for a credit check on cards. These go away quickly and have a low impact on your score, but avoid multiple credit checks in a short amount of time.

RULES FOR USING CREDIT CARDS EFFECTIVELY

Use your credit card to pay for things you would normally purchase, like essential transactions:

- Gas
- Food
- Bills
- Emergencies

Pay off your credit card EVERY *month to avoid interest charges.*

DO NOT USE YOUR CARD FOR NONESSENTIAL TRANSACTIONS LIKE

- Going out to restaurants/bars
- Toys and entertainment
- Things you do not actually need

After about three to six months, apply for another credit card. (Look for one that offers *cash back or benefits* when you use it. *Amazon* has a great one for this.) Split your bills between the two credit cards you decide to use and continue to pay off both cards at the end of the month.

Do not use your cash/income if possible. Just use your cards and pay them off with your income.

Eventually, you will see your credit score climb as you create a positive payment history.

Use a credit monitoring app on your phone and the Internet to learn how to manage credit and build it. I use the Credit Karma app, but there are more options, and even some banks and credit cards offer similar services. These are normally free, so don't pay for one that charges you.

And don't spend more than you make!

Continue this process until you have three credit cards. You will start getting offers for higher lines of credit. It usually starts at $200.

Eventually, you will see much higher dollar amounts offered to you. Take it, but *never spend more than you make!*

As you go through this process, you will see your credit score climb. As your credit climbs, you will get more offers with lower interest rates and higher credit limits. You will want to use the cards that offer you benefits over those that don't, but don't close the accounts you choose not to use anymore.

Once you get to this point, let me know what life looks like for you! Email me at rcsg@changingpatternsinc.org with your story and pictures so we can celebrate your success!

*****

Building credit takes incredible discipline. It is so easy to throw your card down during frivolous times, especially if you are drinking. Watch out for those types of moments. Here are some ways to protect yourself from yourself:

- *Don't take your credit cards with you if you are drinking alcohol.*
- *Avoid buying nonessential items.*
- *Don't use more than 50 percent of your total credit line at any given time.*
- *Don't show off; credit doesn't mean you are rich.*

If you follow these steps, you will position yourself with a level of credit that will balance out your criminal record. Your high credit score will make it easier to rent a home, provide an emergency fund, and open doors for opportunities, like starting a business.

Most people and organizations care more about your credit score than your criminal record, especially when your last conviction is ten years or older. If you did six years in prison as I did, then you are not far off from having your criminal record be less of a factor in situations like renting a home, but your credit score will be imperative to getting approved.

Think of your credit score as your "paperwork" out here. Your credit score determines if you are a "good person." Your credit score is your ticket back to being trusted by organizations who judge you by your paperwork. Your credit score *is* your paperwork out here. Keep your paperwork clean, and you will see it balances out your criminal record.

I saved this section to be last because of its importance. Cherish your credit score. Value it as your ticket to freedom and opportunity!

CONCLUSION

> *Change your mental attitude and the world*
> *around you will change. (Napoleon Hill)*

You are 100 percent responsible for your life. You have the ability to work your way to earning complete freedom. This won't happen in one day. It likely won't happen in one year, but it will happen if you make a personal commitment to change.

Work hard in everything you do, and life will start to present you with trophies of accomplishment, experience, wisdom, and most importantly, freedom.

The day you walk out of prison, you automatically get more choices. As you make choices, which support your goals and desires, you will start to see results, which support your accomplishing those goals and achieving those desires.

The conclusion question is, are those goals and desires ones that are prosocial and healthy?

If so, then this guide will help you.

My request to you is simple: *Share this guide with anyone you know who can use it.* Anyone in transition can use this guide to build a foundation to launch toward their version of freedom.

I believe everyone has the privilege to earn their definition of freedom. It takes hard work and dedication. Freedom is truly earned. Freedom for people like you and me comes when we are willing and committed to changing the patterns that caused us to lose our freedom in the first place. We change those patterns to ones that cause us to *gain* our freedom.

Transition is a tough time for everyone. My hope is this guide will be a resource for you to overcome some of the challenges and that you are able to build a foundation to launch into the life you have always wanted.

The grass IS greener on this side of the fence. Freedom is the greatest thing we can earn, and I look forward to connecting with you as free, returned citizens.

#ChangeThePattern
Our thoughts influence our attitude.
Our attitude fuels our imagination.
Our imagination illustrates the nature of our desires.
The nature of our desires dictates our behavior.
Our behavior is the reason for the life we experience.

Much love and respect,
Frank C. Patka
SID #: 14692795

Rule #76, No excuses. Play like a champion.
(Vince Vaughn, *Wedding Crashers)*

RESOURCES

Sample résumé:

Frank C. Patka IV
PO Box 675 • Bend • OR 97709 • frankpatka@
example.com • 555-555-5555

Sales Executive
Customer Service • Closer • Public Speaker

Performance Profile

Enthusiastic, personable, and committed to professional growth; able to prioritize multiple activities and is a highly reliable self-starter; can be counted on to complete assignments without supervision; has the ability to prioritize multiple activities but can be flexible and is able to adjust to change while showing dedication to the job.

Skills

- Cold-calling
- Market research
- Teamwork
- Communications
- Leadership
- Organization

Experience

Experimac, Bend, OR 2017–Present
A local company that buys, sells, trades, and repairs all Apple products.

- Diagnosed and did troubleshooting on mobile devices
- Repaired iPhones, iPads, iPods, and Android mobile devices; customers received quality and timely repairs on their mobile devices so they would not be without them for long
- Sales and marketing; outside sales in person, introducing the company to other businesses, and facilitating social media marketing on multiple platforms, which increased visibility and revenue.

PerfectVision Enterprise, Bend, OR 2016–Present
Owner
A problem-solving company that focuses on helping small businesses grow their top line by organizing sales, implementing systems, leading goal-setting exercises, and assisting in culture-changing activities.

- Built a new customer base for clients, prepared sales scripts, did cold-call/outside sales, and organized the CRM. Past clients saw a 40 percent increase in revenue over the first year, doubled their second year, and are projected to quadruple by end of 2018.
- Managed the financial data of the company while analyzing clients' budgets and financial practices.
- Assisted in the hiring process and created new-hire manuals for a massage clinic and B2B printer supply vendor.
- Led social media marketing for the purpose of creating top-of-mind publicity, and coached effective marketing techniques so clients created more qualified lead traffic to websites and stores.

El Rodeo, Bend, OR 2016–Present
Bartender

Mexican restaurant and local landmark, serving quality food, a friendly atmosphere, and top-shelf margaritas.

- Serve food and alcohol to patrons
- Monitor alcohol consumption
- Create a fun, friendly atmosphere with entertaining conversation

Springtime Landscape and Irrigation, Bend, OR 2006–2009
Landscape Technician

A landscape, irrigation, and construction company that offers landscaping and maintenance services to both commercial and personal customers.

- Maintained customers' lawns and gardens; kept their lawns looking green and lush; kept gardens weed-free and blossoming; pruned when needed. Had happy customers and beautiful yards. Many return customers each year.
- Troubleshooting problems and relating to the customer about the problem and potential solutions; I would help understand how the customer felt about the problem and figure out the best plan of action or person to solve the problem. I had some successful experiences solving problems with customers to create good customer service results.
- Stepped up to be the crew foreman when ours could not be there; I would lead, direct, drive and work alongside our team to make sure we were continuing to be productive even though the boss was gone. I never had trouble getting the team to work, and we always finished the day accomplishing our service commitments.

Education

Defy Ventures

Nationally recognized entrepreneurship training program and start-up incubator for returning citizens; featured in *The New Yorker, The New York Times, The Wall Street Journal* magazine, and Forbes, NY

- Engage in hands-on leadership, management, and entrepreneurial training, which develops team-building skills, emotional intelligence, innovative spirit, and endurance
- Compete in Shark Tank-style business plan competitions, judged by VCs, Fortune 500 executives, entrepreneurs, and investors.
- Invest fifteen hours/week in training; receive mentoring from top investors and executives

Central Oregon Community College, Madras, OR

One-year certificate in welding and manufacturing

- Worked part-time while taking forty-five credits
- Forty-five credits completed; coursework includes: MFG 100–202, Math 85, MFG 107–284

Notables

- **TEDx Bend Presenter**—5/13/2017
- **Boxer and Boxing Coach**—2000–2016
- **One Year Welding Certificate** (COCC)—2013–2014
- **Launch Your Business Certificate** (SBDC/COCC)—2014

****

Five questions that make networking easy

Question #1: "What do you do for work, fun, the weekend, excitement, Frank?"

What we "do for _________" is something we all use as an identifying label and an easy question to ask strangers. What we do for work; what we do for fun; what we do for (fill in the blank)— these are social norm questions and a safe way to get started.

Of course, don't forget to use their name.

Asking the "what do you do for _________" question is also a great lead-in for beginning networkers because it is low risk when it comes to having a conversation. It's hard to find yourself in a difficult conversation when you ask one of the most generic conversation starters.

Asking about what one does for work is mostly used to qualify someone at a networking event anyway.

Why am I promoting a "generic conversation starter"?" Because it's a great question to learn about someone. Remember what effective networking is really about: IT'S NOT ABOUT YOU, IT'S ABOUT OTHERS.

What better way to start learning about someone you met than a safe but informative question?

Use the tips. LISTEN! Don't just ask the question and take a break while they are talking. How many times have you been asked a question by someone and started to answer only to feel they stopped listening or you see them look at the phone?

Once you find out what they do, say for work, you can follow up to learn more.

Follow-up questions:

- How did you get into that industry, position, or job?
- Why did you choose that profession?
- What is your favorite part of your job?

Listen for relatable topics to engage in.

Question #2: "Where are you from? Are you from here? How long have you lived here?"

Another safe but informative question is asking about where someone is from. This can give you an opportunity to connect based on location or learn about an area you are not familiar with.

Most people are happy to tell you about where they are from or where they have moved from or that they are one of the rare townies. Okay, not everyone, but enough people understand the conversation to have it part of your networking process.

This question has easy follow-up questions, which will help you find relatable topics or interesting things to learn.

Follow-up questions:

- What brought you here?
- What do you miss most about where you came from?
- What is your favorite thing about here?

Question #3: "Who is a good referral for you? Who are you looking to connect with? Who is your ideal customer?"

A great way to build a relationship with someone while networking is to ask them who their ideal customer is or who they are looking to connect with. Since *great networking is about the other person*, this question really allows you to focus on what they need.

You will earn credibility with them through this simple but rare question.

Think about it: How many people ask you who is a good referral for your business?

Follow-up questions:

- What is the best way to connect them with you? How do I refer you to them?
- What services do you provide to them?
- What should I listen for to know they would be a good referral?

Question #4: "What do you like to do for fun? What hobbies do you have? What sports do you like? What are your favorite activities?"

What people do for extracurricular activities, fun, and relief is a great way to find relatable topics. Who knows, you may wind up finding a pickleball partner or hiking friend that turns into a business connection.

No matter the result, the reason is about building relationships because life is truly about relationships.

Follow-up questions:

- How did you get into that (sport/activity)?
- Why do you like it?
- How do I get into it?
- Where is the best place to __________?
- Who is your favorite team? Who is your favorite player?

Question #5: "What is your endgame? What is 'success'? What are your goals? How do you want to be remembered?"

These questions are more intimate than the first four and are best asked after a level of credibility and trust is established.

Because of the level of intimacy of these questions, they will give you answers which will connect you to the individual's true purpose in life.

At the end of the day, aren't we all striving for some purpose in life?

This question also gives you a filter on who you are talking to. Effective networking is learning about the other person. This does not mean every "other person" is someone you need in your life.

Before diving into these questions, take an audit of yourself. Ask yourself, *"Why are you initiating conversation and asking questions to learn about others?"* What is your purpose in asking?

This self-audit will give you an opportunity to be clear in your intention as you build a more intimate relationship.

I am interested in people, and I thrive on connecting. However, I also network to see who is a right fit for my direction.

There are almost eight billion people in this world. Not everyone is meant to be in my network. The best way to find out if someone is a good fit for my direction or if I am a good fit for their direction is to learn about their endgame.

Follow-up questions:

- What puts you on this path?
- What does success look like to you?
- What is your vision?
- How are you working toward accomplishing this now?

Summary:

Networking is not as scary, hard, or selective as we think. The best way to network is to approach it with the intention to learn about others. The easiest way to learn about others is to ask questions, listen to them, and of course, remember their name.

My encouragement is to be an effective networker and learn about other people. You will actually make a difference in others' lives just by following these steps. How crazy is that? You will be remembered as a good listener, appreciated as a person, and likely be given opportunities to help others (and make money doing it) because you

1. Initiated a conversation with the intent to learn
2. Learned someone's name and remembered it
3. Asked questions and engaged in relatable conversation

Mentor assessment questions:

Write your answers to better assess what you want out of a mentor.
What do you want a mentor to have achieved?
What areas in life are they successful in?
What skills would you like them to teach you?
How available are they, or how frequent would you like to meet?
How do you want them to hold you accountable?

One-Week Schedule

Time	Mon	Tue	Wed	Thr	Fri	Sat	Sun
5am 6am							
7am 8am							
9am 10am							
11am 12							
1pm 2pm							
3pm 4pm							
5pm 6pm							

Time	Mon	Tue	Wed	Thr	Fri	Sat	Sun
5am							
6am							
7pm							
8pm							
9pm							
10pm							

ACKNOWLEDGMENTS

Here's to those who made a direct contribution to the making of this book. Without you, I've got nothing. I guarantee I forgot plenty of people. And if you are still in my life, then please let me know. I will correct the mistake. Thank you to everyone in my life.

*****

In January 2010, I started my journey into the Oregon prison system.

Mom, during my time, you taught me that every time I get in trouble, I push back my freedom further. It's not about what little I lost (I had nothing to lose), it was about how much further I pushed away what I wanted. You kept me from getting into too much trouble when you asked me not to screw up after going minimum. I leaned on my promise to you a lot during those three years. I love you, Mom.

Dad, you came to visit me on an average of more than two times a month. I'd bet once a month when I was at EO. I tell people we became friends because of you showing up consistently and being willing to sit uncomfortably, playing chess after our first visits, including hanging up the phone. Thank you for being my dad. Of course, I love you too!

Mr. Phillip Morrison, you asked me one of the most important questions I've ever been asked, and your timing was impeccable. That question: *"Do you want to keep doing this prison shit, or do you want to learn something cool?"* Thank you for seeing in me what I had yet to see in myself. Thank you for being willing to teach me. Thank you for inspiring me to think beyond what I believed was true. You changed my life.

Janet Narum, you taught me that it is better to have integrity and be misunderstood than to compromise under pressure. Thank you for being awesome and weird. Thank you for letting me help others get their GED.

Meredith Allen, "*Yo*," you influenced me more than anyone in leadership and character. You showed me that standing for something good is more important than what others say. You helped me become a leader. You sacrificed more for people in prison than anyone I have ever met. You are an example others should follow when it comes to truly motivating rehabilitation in people who are in prison. If the system offered you the opportunity to lead, your leadership would reduce recidivism.

Mr. Hormann, thank you for revealing to me that there are staff in the correctional system who are trustworthy and truly want to help adults in custody change their prior harmful habits into pro-social behaviors. Thank you for putting your reputation on the line and taking shots from all sides to establish and lead the innovative *Prosocial Movement* at Deer Ridge Correctional Institution.

Mr. Bowman, for treating people in prison like people—thank you for providing a venue for convicts to learn how to be productive workers in the community.

Thank you to all the staff and volunteers who helped me and other adults in custody consider a more prosocial way of living and behaving.

Cheers to Diablo, Hollywood, Allen, and Ben for bossing up and founding a movement that has lasted longer than any of us imagined. No one can relate to the weight of responsibility we chose to carry. You are all warriors in my eyes and will never be forgotten. Much love and respect.

Tank, you played an important role, which is why I am mentioning you.

PeeWee, thank you for having my back and being a good friend.

Rafa, you know what's up. Double mention because you are one of the best. I'll flinch for you any day. I miss ya, buddy. Come check out the boxing gym some time.

Kwajo Assuman, the rock of Defining Your Chief Aim. I don't know where the program is as of now, but I can tell you, our curriculum and class were taught long after I was released. I don't know how many lives changed, but I know mine did for the better because of what you and I accomplished. Thank you.

Carol Freed, you were with me through my entire prison sentence. You wrote me letters, sent cartoons and jokes and pictures. You made my day every day I received a letter. I loved our visits… more so after I got out. You invested in me. You continue to hold me accountable. Thank you.

Kelsey Hulbert, from the time we started talking to each other as adults, you ask me what I am doing for self-care. I don't know how many years it has taken me, but I am finally starting to understand the difference between *self-care* and *having fun*. I have yet figured out this "balanced lifestyle" yet, but thank you for always caring about my well-being.

Caleb, wish you were here. You'd love this.

In November 2015, I started my re-entry experience. My sister, Kelsie, and brother-in-law, Jeff, were gracious and trusting enough to allow me to live with them and my freshly made nephew, Peter. The thanks I owe them could never be repaid. Because of their generosity, I was able to live in a safe place with opportunities to learn and create. Changing Patterns would not exist without the hours of shoveling manure out of the paddock. I love you.

Dad, you get a second mention for being my first employer and trusting me to stir the pot in your business. I am grateful the results were positive because we were both living on a prayer.

Mom, yes, without you, I would not have been able to drive to Dan's birthday party and feel the welcoming love of friends that are family. I wouldn't have been able to afford that eight-hundred-dollar car with windows that didn't work. You continue to be a major supporter in my life. You are the best.

Jerry Schulz, where would I be without you? Not here. This book would not exist. I might not even exist. I could write a chapter about your influence in this book. This book was written in your house because you and Char believe in me. I love you. Thank you.

Gneel, my friend, my brother since we were knee-high to a grasshopper, you know how much I love you, so please don't make this weird. Just let me move on and recognize other people. It was hard enough to wait this long to mention you so no one would think I was playing favorites. Dude, writing acknowledgments is hard. All I am doing is realizing how many people I am not going to mention while listening to Too Many Zooz. Check them out. Pretty dope.

Sanda Costello, you were willing to hire this f———up after a history of bad experiences. Not only did you pay for my attorney but you also paid for being my friend for the rest of your life. Feel free to send me an invoice. You taught me more than I'll ever admit. I love you!

Tim Nihoul, meeting you brought me into BBG, which has provided me with more opportunities than ever. I'm still earning opportunities because of your offering a meetup to play Cashflow. You have the superpower of connecting people.

Michelle Mora, you checked me when I started smoking weed and screwed up my business. You kept me focused on my TED Talk, which would have been trash without your positive influence. Thank you for being an amazing friend and sharing many moments. You have a lifelong friend in me. I love you.

Kelly Sheets! You told me to write a book, and I did. What should I do next? After my terrifying speech at City Club, you welcomed me back to the community in a way that gave me the confidence to be open about being a returning citizen. That confidence revealed to me a lesson of how powerful authenticity can be. Thank you.

Joanne Matthews, without you, my TED Talk would have been trash too. Seriously, this woman made me when it comes to real public speaking. Toastmasters was my elementary school and junior high. Joanne, you brought me through the high school of speaking to being a legitimate public speaker. And then you continued to mentor me as a board member. My hero.

Lewis "the Legend" Sperber, you are one of the most significant people in my life, my friend. Thank you for being you. I have learned more from you about human beings than anyone I know. I am always your friend.

Heather Fitch and Stefanie Seibold, without you two, we would not have come as far as we did in providing healthy opportunities for those getting out of prison. You gave me opportunities to speak in front of people I may never have without you. You showed me what a strong and effective team looks like, and I am grateful for our time together working on the ECO System.

To all the team members of the Essential Connections Opportunity System, thank you for investing your time in offering education to those who are preparing for release. A special thank you to the founding members of the cohort: Joe Millazo, Loren Peterson, Penny Newton, Christian Moller Anderson, Dana Dunlap, and Ryan Huff.

Teresa Laursen, thank you for buying into the cause of supporting returning citizens in their re-entry back to the community with me on the board and editing the book.

John Hummel, thank you for taking time out of your busy schedule to support ideas like Changing Patterns, and thank you for your dedication to influencing positive change in our criminal justice system. The world needs more people like you.

To every person who has been part of Changing Patterns, thank you so much for investing your time, money, and patience in dealing with me and my ideas. Thank you for believing in me.

Nathan Mansfield, your greatest influence on me has been how hard you strive to provide for those you love. I respect and love you. Thank you for letting me live with you and being part of your family.

Garzas, I have adopted you. Neither Ricky nor I knew what would come from this relationship. Neither of us ever imagined a life like it is, and I am so grateful to have you both in my life. Jamie, you have added months, maybe even years, to my life and brought me and my friend closer together. Ricky, thank you for going the other way and making a life where you can provide opportunities for others. You are my favorite roommate and the best place I have ever lived as an adult. What's for dinner?

Firo, what would I have done without you? First, thanks to David Robles for loving me enough to bring me into your family and your dear, Rudy Arias Jr., a.k.a. Firo, a.k.a. ________ (fill in the blank). Rudy, thank you for providing me with ways to make income, a place to live, someone to talk success with, the 2020 10X Growth Con, and all our future endeavors.

There is only one Lit AF, and that is you. I'll wash your dishes and clean your house for the rest of our lives if you'll have me. I'm making a personal commitment to forever be your househusband. I am grateful to be able to close out life with you. Capital L for Cheryl.

Ryan McCrone, where would the world be without environmental debates around firepits in the backyard? It would be less interesting. Thank you for being an amazing friend. Your superpower is connecting people.

Hoffman, Matthew, my future financial advisor and present confidant, neither of us know what friends we are to each other, but we both knew there is always someone to call. We need more talks about sociology, and you have yet to play me in pickleball.

Chris Kearns, thank you for helping me get back on track with my health. Thank you for promoting sober living and helping me get strong enough not to feel weak.

Paul Abbott, thank you for being willing to hire this former inmate and giving me a chance to participate in your business.

Raymond Shields, we met once. You were my uber driver who picked me up when Allen and I got into a drunken argument, and I chose to stay in a hotel that night. I bought your book, *It Should Have Been Common Sense*, and read it that night in the hotel as I promised. Reading your book helped me overcome a long writing drought and motivated me to finish the job—this book. Thank you.

Ryan Costello, you helped me believe I could be influential in this prison-incarceration subject and help change things for the better. I miss pontificating over drinks and how every imagination and situation ended in tragic laughter.

Jason Adams, thank you for investing in me. Thank you for giving me the opportunity to learn new skills and gain business experience I would otherwise not be able to without your willingness to give me a chance.

Leslie Renaud Kuther, you are the best manager I ever worked under. If I could pay you to manage my life, I would. I trust you more than I could ever show. Thank you, to you and Cliff, for being stand-up people and a positive influence in my life.

Mike Guest and the *Bend Rubber Stamp & Printing* team, thank you for working with me in printing the first copies of this book.

I'm glad you are part of this journey.

Thank you, Mike Patterson, for bringing me into your life. I hope I have been as much of a positive part of yours as you have been to mine. *I am grateful you are still here* (had to add that last line). And thank you for introducing me to your son, Michalis Patterson.

Michalis (Mike) Patterson, I love you, man. I'm not always in your life, but you are always in mine. Your music is in my life's playlist. Your album, *Recycled Experiences*, is not only one of my favorite albums but the soundtrack that influenced much of this book. I spent thirty-eight hours over three days listening to *Recycled Experiences* while I revised this book in South Carolina. I only hope this book influences someone like you have influenced me.

Sean Williams, thank you for recruiting me and making me feel like I am valuable. Thank you for trusting me with your business. Thank you for introducing me to the greatest team to work with: Skinny Vinny, Mike the Weatherman, Westside Cory, Scootch McDuck, Claybo, and my favorite landscaper, the high watermark of my workday, Sky Wilgus.

Truett J. Watts and Ronald Allen Roper, you are my two best friends from prison. Because of you, I was able to stay a positive course in a negative environment. Without you two, I would not have gone through my prison experience as productive. You were two of my positive influences.

Allen, thank you for getting out of prison and sticking with determination to build the life you want. Thank you for having a healthy place to host me so I could finish this book. Thank you for being one of the best friends a guy could have.

Truett, this book was written for you and all of us. Welcome home. Welcome to freedom now and for life.

John Johnson, you played an integral part in my becoming the man I am today. Your input in my life and in this book has been invaluable and will continue as we grow. Welcome home. Now come write your book with us.

There are many more who have influenced this book that I have not mentioned. Nothing I have done was by myself. I truly love you all, but I need to finish and publish this book. Stay tuned for more…

SOURCES

1. https://worldpopulationreview.com/countryrankings/incarceration-rates-by-country
2. https://www.bbc.com/news/world-us-canada-46471444
3. *Think and Grow Rich* by Napoleon Hill
4. https://www.forbes.com/sites/jeannemeister/2012/08/14/the-future-of-work-job-hopping-is-thenew-normal-for-millennials/?sh=454e69c213b8
5. https://frankchazpatka.blogspot.com/2020/03/5-tips-and-5-questions-to-network.html

Motivated, hardworking, innovative, driven to succeed…

After serving seventy months in prison for armed robbery, Frank Patka became a returning citizen and started a new life with his estranged community.

Frank was able to navigate the barriers and obstacles of re-entry because of securing fundamental needs, like safe housing, employment, transportation, and a healthy support system. However, many of his friends and fellow returning citizens did not share Frank's experience after release.

After watching his friends succumb to addiction, go back to prison, and even lose their lives, Frank realized many people getting out of prison are disconnected from the reality of how to live.

In 2017, Frank founded Changing Patterns, a nonprofit with a mission to support citizens returning home from incarceration to become healthy, well-respected members of their families, and productive members of our communities.

Changing Patterns began to focus on providing personal mentoring for returning citizens and act as a networking opportunity for clients to connect with community resources as the mentoring program was rolling out COVID hit the United States, and everyone's lives changed.

Bursting with energy and motivation backed by years of research and personal experience, Frank wrote *Returning Citizen's Survival Guide* during COVID of the shutdown. The book was written for people who are incarcerated within one year until release and for the purpose of better preparing them to be successful in their re-entry.

This is his first book and is currently working with his team in Oregon to develop more material and support returning citizens with their nonprofit, Changing Patterns.

You can contact Frank and his team at info@changingpatternsinc.org.